A GLOSSARY OF US POLITICS
AND GOVERNMENT

Politics Glossaries

Series Editor: Keith Faulks

This series introduces key terms within the core subject areas of politics. The aim is to provide a brief, clear and convenient A–Z guide to the central concepts of the various branches of politics.

The series provides thorough, authoritative and concise reference works which offer clear and consistent coverage of both traditional and contemporary terminology. Students and teachers of politics at all levels of study will find the books invaluable, though the books are aimed primarily at readers new to a subject area. In addition to appealing to mainstream politics students, the series will also appeal to those studying courses in sociology, journalism, media studies and social policy that include elements of politics.

Volumes in the series provide:

- Dedicated coverage of particular topics within politics
- Coverage of key terms and major figures
- Practical examples of the terms defined
- Cross-references to related terms

Titles in the series include:

John Hoffman, *A Glossary of Political Theory*
Alistair Jones, *A Glossary of the European Union*
Alex Thomson, *A Glossary of US Politics and Government*
Duncan Watts, *A Glossary of UK Government and Politics*

A Glossary of US Politics and Government

Alex Thomson

Edinburgh University Press

© Alex Thomson, 2007

Edinburgh University Press Ltd
22 George Square, Edinburgh

Typeset in 10.5/13 Sabon by
Servis Filmsetting Ltd, Manchester, and
printed and bound in Great Britain by
Cox & Wyman Ltd, Reading

A CIP record for this book is
available from the British Library

ISBN 978 0 7486 2804 9 (hardback)
ISBN 978 0 7486 2253 5 (paperback)

Contents

Preface

The United States houses one of the most intricate systems of government in the world, and produces politics of a complex nature. As a result, to understand this political arena, one needs to take on board many variables: the functions of a whole host of individual institutions; key political events that have occurred over some 250 years; individuals who have shaped this history; and the numerous expressions scholars have 'coined' in order to explain this political system. This may seem daunting at first. One has to sort out the **legislative branch** from the **executive branch**, and then work out where the **Supreme Court** resides in this political dispensation. This is before one realises that the **federal government** is only part of the equation, and that there are fifty other sovereign governments in the USA: those belonging to the individual states. And then there are the people and organisations that inhabit this system of government (politicians, political parties, interest groups, government departments, courts, **independent agencies**, and so on). Not to mention methods of representation, in terms of **general elections**, **primary elections**, recall votes, state **initiatives**, lobbying and so forth. One needs some kind of mental map in order to put all these fragments of government and politics back together, to gain an overall picture. Most use the US **constitution** as the starting point for drawing this map. And the constitution itself introduces a plethora of phrases that need to be understood (the **commerce clause**, **denied powers**, **strict construction** – again the list goes on). If you are serious about wanting to comprehend US politics and government there is a lot to learn.

The good news is that assistance is at hand: literally. This book is specifically designed to help you understand the above events, institutions and terminology, and many more key words and phrases besides. It is not a comprehensive and exhaustive twelve-volume encyclopaedia of everything related to US politics and government, nor is it meant to be a substitute for the vast literature of books and articles published on this subject. Additionally, it is not a general political dictionary. There are no non-US-specific entries, such as 'democracy' in general or a broad consideration of 'socialism'. The book is, instead, dedicated to terms that provide a good starting point for a journey into the politics of this part of the world.

A Glossary of US Politics and Government works best when read alongside other texts. It will help newcomers to this subject understand a phrase or concept they come across in their other reading, while more knowledgeable scholars can use the entries in this book to clarify or remind themselves about a term previously encountered. Once you have looked up a word, and satisfied yourself of its meaning, you can then return to studying the key texts. However, having said this, there is nothing to stop you browsing. Inevitably with glossaries, one often finds oneself following a path, with one entry leading to another: **separation of the powers** leads to **Supreme Court,** which leads to *Brown* v. *Board of Education,* 1954, which leads to **civil rights movement,** and so on. Glossary browsing is a great way to build up knowledge of a subject, but remember, the best way to learn is to eventually get back to the key texts! This book is only designed to give snap-shots, helping you digest more comprehensive volumes.

So, what is actually in this book? Well, it is a collection of 500 or so explanations of often-used terms and phrases found in the study of US politics and government. These are listed in strict alphabetical order. The entries have been selected around four themes: institutions, historical events, expressions and personalities. Enough information is given to help one understand an issue, but the entries are deliberately concise in order not to bog the reader down with too many facts and detain them too long. Remember, the book is a companion to other recommended reading, not a substitute for it.

In addition to the 500 or so entries that make up the vast bulk of this book are three appendices: 'US **Presidents** and **Vice Presidents**', 'US Supreme Court **Chief Justices**', and details of the US **Congress** since this body's first session. These tables can be referred to when you need to confirm who was President or Chief Justice when, and which political party controlled the US Congress or the **White House** at a certain point in history. These are the types of sources that even the most experienced scholar of US politics has to turn to every now and then: when they forget which President succeeded William Henry Harrison in 1841, for example, after he died in office. In times of need or forgetfulness, we all need *aide memoires*, such as the present book.

I also thought it would be useful to include the URLs of websites at the end of selected glossary entries. These are the official home-pages of the institutions concerned: the US **Senate**, for example, or the **National Rifle Association**. These URLs, however, have been confined to official sites. Readers may wish to search beyond these particular web pages, seeking a more critical view of these institutions. Similarly, one or two entries include further reading recommendations. Such recommendations have only been given when a specific book is mentioned in the text. Rather than overwhelm readers with several suggested books for each individual glossary entry, it would probably be better to start with a holistic view, and consult a couple of good text books instead. Two volumes, in particular, come highly recommended: George McKay's *American Politics and Society* (Oxford: Blackwell,

2005), and *The Irony of Democracy*, written by Thomas R. Dye and Harmon Zeigler (Belmont, CA: Wadsworth, 2005). The former is a good solid introductory text, written by a British-based author, useful to American and non-American scholars alike, while the latter is a (self sub-titled) 'uncommon introduction' to the US system, offering a slightly more radical twist.

To assist the reader, all the entries in the glossary are cross-referenced. If you need further information about a topic, you can simply follow the cross-references to other sections of the book. Any entry in this glossary that appears within the description of another word or phrase is **highlighted** like so.

If you use the above tools, what starts out to be a daunting and complex task, with a bit of effort, soon becomes easier and more straightforward. For, although the US system is intricate, it is also one of the most logical political dispensations in the world. I hope this glossary will help you to unravel this logic, and above all, I hope this book contributes to your enjoyment of this political system.

My thanks go to Roy Perry, Jacques Gallagher, Janice Ellis, and Keith Faulks for their suggestions which have improved this book.

ART
Manchester, 2006

A Glossary of US Politics and Government

A

abolitionists Those seeking to abolish slavery. Although
there had always been voices raised against the institution of slavery, the opposition campaign became more
prominent from the 1830s onwards. Abolition was now
firmly on the political agenda of the United States, if by
no means the majority view. Newspapers such as
William Lloyd Garrison's *The Liberator* and Frederick
Douglass' *Northern Star* popularised the movement's
demands. Many abolitionists were involved in an
'underground railway', a network of paths and safe-
houses helping slaves to escape to Canada, and freedom.
It would eventually take the **civil war** to bring about the
abolitionists' demands. President Abraham **Lincoln**
made his '**Emancipation Proclamation**' in 1863, and the
end of slavery was confirmed by the **Thirteenth
Amendment** to the US **constitution** in 1865.

affirmative action Measures that positively discriminate, providing opportunities to previously disadvantaged groups
in society. After the **civil rights movement** had won victories securing equal political rights and desegregation for
African-Americans, attention began to turn to addressing
social inequalities. Discrimination had denied African-
Americans, and other minorities, opportunities in the
workplace and access to public services. Affirmative
action is about redressing this imbalance. The Medical
School of the University of California at Davis in the mid-
1970s, for example, attempted to increase the number of
its 'minority' graduates by setting admissions quotas.
Sixteen of one hundred places were to be reserved for
minority students. However, Allan Bakke, a white appli-
cant, was denied admission to the School in both 1973 and
1974, even though his test scores and grades were better

than most of those admitted through the affirmative action program. His case went to the **Supreme Court,** and in the judgment *Regents of the University of California* v. *Bakke,* 1978 the justices ruled that such a rigid quota system was unconstitutional: Bakke himself had been discriminated against. Legally, affirmative action cannot reward an individual simply because of their race. A student from a minority group may be preferred over one from the majority with better grades because of their unique character or background, or in order to create diversity on a course, but not solely on racial grounds. Each case has to be judged individually on its own merits.

AFL-CIO see **American Federation of Labor and Congress of Industrial Organizations**

Agnew, Spiro (1918–96) A former Republican **governor** of Maryland, Spiro Agnew (born Spiro Anagnostopoulos) was **Vice President** of the United States between 1969 and 1973. He resigned from this post as a result of tax irregularities and bribery allegations. He later pleaded 'no contest' to criminal charges of tax evasion. His resignation triggered the provisions of the **Twenty-fifth Amendment** to the US **constitution,** whereby senator, and later **President,** Gerald **Ford,** became Richard **Nixon's** Vice President. The discredit Agnew bestowed upon this administration was a forerunner to the **Watergate** scandal that eventually led to Nixon's own resignation in 1974.

Air Force One The aeroplane dedicated to transporting the **President** and presidential staff on official business. 'Air Force One' is the radio call-sign used when the President is on board.

amendments, constitutional see **constitutional amendments**

American exceptionalism The idea that the United States has a unique, relatively homogeneous society and culture, based upon ideas of liberty, individualism and populism. Scholars and politicians alike have used this notion of exceptionalism to explain various aspects of American history: the failure, for example, of this country to develop deeper social fault lines between the interests of capital and labour. This perceived exceptionalism has prompted many Americans to believe they have a superior culture to others around the world. Most Americans certainly consider the US to be a unique bastion of freedom, while many contend the values of this exceptionalism should be exported abroad.

American Federation of Labor and Congress of Industrial Organizations (AFL-CIO) The AFL-CIO was created in 1955 by the merger of the American Federation of Labor and the Congress of Industrial Organizations to form the most influential trades union institution in the United States. Individual unions affiliated to this organisation currently represent a total of 9 million American workers (including some in Canada, Mexico and Panama). As well as addressing workers' interests at the shop-floor level, this organisation, although not as powerful as comparable European union federations, actively lobbies and sponsors candidates at all levels of US government. Internal disputes have occasionally weakened the AFL-CIO. In 1957, for example, the **Teamsters**, the United States biggest union, were expelled from the organisation after allegations of corruption and labour racketeering, while the United Automobile Workers withdrew in 1968, due to complaints that the AFL-CIO was not radical enough. Both these unions reaffiliated during the 1980s. Despite these reaffiliations, the AFL-CIO has seen a declining membership since a peak of 17 million represented workers in the late 1970s. In 2005, the organisation hit another crisis with the Teamsters yet again disaffiliating, along with several other large unions, seeking to create a more modern labour movement.

Website: http://www.aflcio.org

anti-federalists Those who opposed the **ratification** of the US **constitution** in the late 1780s. Although many of these individuals conceded that the United States needed a more centralised government than had been the case under the **Articles of Confederation**, they considered the constitution negotiated by the **Founding Fathers** to cede too much power from the states to the new **federal government**. They were particularly concerned about the role of the **President** as **Commander in Chief** and chief diplomat; the power of the judiciary; the federal government's ability to raise taxes; Congress' rights with the **implied powers**; and that federal legislators would be too distant from their constituents. Despite these fears, ultimately, federalist, not anti-federalist, arguments prevailed. Only two of the thirteen states voted against ratification (Rhode Island and North Carolina), and by 1790 all thirteen states had adopted the constitution as penned in Philadelphia. Anti-federalist arguments addressing the constitution's lack of protection for individual liberty, however, were recognised. In 1791, the first ten amendments to the US constitution, collectively known as the **Bill of Rights**, were ratified, providing such protection.

appellant A party who appeals the decision of the lower court of law to a higher authority.

appellate court A court of law that has the power to review the decision of a lower court. The **Supreme Court** is the highest appellate authority in the United States.

appointment power The US **constitution** gives the **President** of the United States the right to staff the offices of the **executive branch** within the **federal government.** The president will select those who will serve in the higher-ranking positions within his or her administration (such as **cabinet** members, ambassadors, military officers, and over 1,000 deputy and assistant secretaries). Lower-ranking officials within the executive branch will be employed by department heads, under the authority of the President. The President's appointment powers also require the **chief executive** to select justices to the **Supreme Court** and lower courts, when these positions become vacant. In order to preserve the system of **checks and balances,** presidential nominations for these posts are usually subject to **confirmation** by the US **Senate. Governors,** as chief executives within state governmental systems, hold similar appointment powers.

appropriation The allocation of money for a specific purpose. All spending by the **federal government** has to have received prior approval by the US **Congress.** Resources available to the **executive branch** will usually be allocated by the **House of Representatives Committee on Appropriations.**

Appropriations Committee see **House of Representatives Committee on Appropriations**

arms for hostages scandal see **Irangate**

Articles of Confederation Effectively, the initial **constitution** of the United States, regulating political cooperation between the ex-colonies from 1781 to 1789. The Articles were drawn up in the early revolutionary period by a committee of the **Continental Congress**. Fearful of a strong central government, the Articles carefully outlined what the national government could and could not do, making sure that the rights of the thirteen states remained paramount. Although the national government could raise an army, regulate a postal service, mint a national currency, and oversee the expansion into the western territories, the states devolved little of their sovereignty. There would be no tax-raising powers for the new central government (and thus no independent source of revenue), nor provision for a separate **executive** or **judicial branch**. Similarly, the United States could only declare war or agree foreign treaties if nine of the thirteen states approved the national government's decision to do so. After considerable debate, the Articles of Confederation came into force upon their **ratification** by Maryland in 1781. Despite this document's aim of creating a 'perpetual union' between the thirteen states, the Articles failed to underpin an effective confederation. The national government lacked power to settle trading disputes between the individual states, or to represent them in the international area. States repeatedly failed to fund the central government adequately, in particular preventing the United States from honouring its debts to those who had assisted the **War of Independence**. Realising that a stronger national government was required, the Articles of Confederation were superseded by the **Constitution** of the United States in 1789.

Attorney General The primary legal advisor to a government. In the federal system, the US Attorney General is also the administrative head of the Department of Justice. The post was established by the Judiciary Act of 1789 at the request of **President** George **Washington**. As well as being

a key post within the **federal government,** each individual
state also has its own Attorney General.
Website: http://www.usdoj.gov/ag/index.html

B

Balanced Budget and Emergency Deficit Control Act, 1985
see **national debt**

Bay of Pigs An invasion of Cuba, by Cuban exiles, planned
and funded by the administrations of Dwight D.
Eisenhower and John F. **Kennedy.** The US sought to over-
throw the socialist regime of Fidel Castro, and establish
a pro-western regime in Havana. This 1961 invasion
failed catastrophically and severely embarrassed the
Kennedy Administration.

bellwether state An individual state that reflects the political
outlook of the nation as a whole. For example, if the citizens of Florida narrowly voted in favour of a **Republican
Party** presidential candidate at a **general election,** and this
Republican nominee did indeed narrowly take the **White
House** after all the votes nationwide were counted,
Florida would be termed a bellwether state. The word
bellwether derives from the name given to the leading
sheep of a flock, which traditionally wore a bell, encour-
aging others to follow it.

Beltway see **Washington Beltway**

bi-cameral legislature A two-chambered parliament. The
bi-cameral system traditionally evolved to represent two
different interests in the legislative process. In the case of
the United Kingdom, there is a House of Lords, originally

established to reflect the views of landed society, and a House of Commons, representing other classes. In the US **Congress,** the two chambers are the **Senate** and the **House of Representatives.** The Senate was originally established to represent the interests of the states, while the House was to reflect popular opinion.

Bill of Rights The collective name given to the first ten amendments to the US **constitution.** During the **ratification** process of the original constitution, in the late 1780s, **anti-federalists,** and others, argued that this document did not make enough provision for individual rights. There was a danger that too much power would flow to the new **federal government,** at the expense of the states and individual citizens. Therefore, in order to secure ratification, it was agreed that additional clauses addressing these concerns would be tabled with all due haste. Ratification of ten **constitutional amendments** was completed by the states during 1791.

Collectively, the Bill of Rights deters governments in the United States from attempting to legislate away individual freedoms. It identifies certain inalienable rights enjoyed by all US citizens: the so-called **denied powers.** The First Amendment, for example, states that Congress cannot pass laws that curtail Americans' right of free speech, freedom of association, or the ability to practise religion.

The Bill of Rights also identifies certain standards that governments in the United States have to adhere to when dealing with their citizens. Legally, for example, there must be 'probable cause' before individuals are arrested or have their property searched by the authorities (Fourth Amendment). Similarly, citizens have a right to the 'due process of law', including trial by jury, not being tried for the same crime twice, the right to silence and legal representation, and not being forced to stand witness against themselves (amendments five, six and seven). Amendment eight protects criminals from excessive legal recourse when found guilty, including 'crewel and unusual punishments'.

Amendments two and three reflect the era in which the Bill of Rights was penned. Individuals are protected from governments unreasonably billeting soldiers in private property, while citizens are encouraged to form militias to provide for the nation's security. Controversially in the modern era, the Second Amendment also permits individuals the right to 'keep and bear arms'. What was deemed essential for militias and national security in the eighteenth century is now seen by some as a scourge of US society. Today, many interpret this amendment as authorising US citizens to own private weapons.

The idea that the Bill of Rights was about creating **limited government,** where powers reserved to individuals and the states cannot be abridged by the federal government, is confirmed in amendments nine and ten. Amendment nine makes clear that the **enumerated rights** articulated in the constitution should not be regarded by the federal government to be the sum total of individual rights in the United States, while the Tenth Amendment categorically asserts that any power not specifically delegated to the federal government by the constitution remains reserved respectively to the states or the people. With the Bill of Rights appended to the original constitution in 1791, the above provisions resulted in anti-federalists having many of their demands to curtail the power of the federal government met.

Bipartisan Campaign Reform Act, 2002 Legislation addressing the use of **soft money** in election campaigns. Although earlier legislation (see **Federal Election Campaign Act, 1971**) had attempted to restrict the sums federal candidates could spend on campaigns, loopholes had been exploited and considerable amounts of soft money continued to be spent by or on behalf of campaigns. In particular, the **Supreme Court** decision of *Buckley* v. *Valeo*, **1976** created a supportive environment for soft money. The Bipartisan Campaign Reform Act (also known as 'McCain-Feingold' after its **Senate** sponsors) closed several of these loopholes. Similarly, the act provides for a stricter legal definition of what an election campaign advertisement is. Before, as long as an advertisement did not overtly call upon the public to vote for a specific candidate, it could be classed as an 'issue ad' rather than one associated with a particular campaign. Elections in the 1990s, as a result, became typified by numerous negative **issue advertisements** being broadcast, criticising opposition candidates, as these could be paid for by soft money. Since the legislation, any advertisement aired within thirty days of a **primary election** or sixty days of a **general election**, which is targeted at a voting constituency, now constitutes an electioneering communication. In order to offer a degree of compensation for the loss of this soft money, the sum of *hard money* that individual citizens and groups can donate to a campaign was doubled. As a result of McCain-Feingold, the 2004 general election saw candidates concentrating on raising record amounts of *hard money* to pay for their campaigns, and less influence being bought with soft money. Controversy continued to surround the use of soft money, however, with the growth of **527 groups**.

bipartisanship Where Republicans and Democrats come together, setting aside party interests, to work for the common good.

Black Panther Party Founded in 1966, this party originated as a self-help movement organised amongst

African-Americans in Oakland, California. Members patrolled the ghettos of this city protecting residents from instances of police brutality. The Black Panthers later developed into a radical 'black power' party, with Marxist leanings. They advocated, amongst other policies, the exemption of black Americans from compulsory military service, and the payment of compensation to all African-Americans for years of exploitation at the hands of their white compatriots. The Black Panthers also organised a number of social programmes amongst African-American communities, including the distribution of food to the poor. At its height, in the late 1960s, the Black Panther Party was active in a number of cities across the United States, and had some 2,000 members. The party's advocacy of practising armed self-defence, and harassment by local police forces, however, led to a number of shoot-outs, and members being imprisoned. These events effectively ended the Black Panther Party's political potency in the early 1970s.

blanket primary A **primary election** where candidates from all parties are on the same ballot paper. Normally, voters are asked to participate in a ballot involving candidates from just one party (a **closed primary**).

block grant A sum of money provided by the **federal government** to state and local governments, or other organisations, accompanied by only broad specifications on how these funds should be spent. A block grant may be given for welfare or housing provision, for example, but recipients will have considerable latitude as to which specific services this money is allocated. With support for **new federalism** growing since the 1970s, block grants have gradually become a more popular way of allocating federal money to the states. The autonomy the states have in spending these funds, to a degree, negates the danger of federal dominance. However, it does remain the case that the states rely heavily on federal revenue to balance their budgets.

Blue Dog Democrats A group of conservative, southern **Democratic Party** members of **Congress** who supported, across party lines, the economic policies of the **Republican Party President** Ronald **Reagan** during the 1980s. The blue dog moniker is a derivation of the earlier term **yellow dog Democrat** combined with references to the work of the artist George Rodrigue, well known in Louisiana for paintings featuring an unusual blue dog. The Blue Dog Democrat group can be seen as descendents of the **boll weevils**, conservative, traditional Democrats who occasionally have more in common with moderate Republicans than they do with the northern, more liberal wing of their own party.

blue state A state where the majority of the electorate support the **Democratic Party**. Given that the United States has a **two-party system,** results of an election are often portrayed on a national map where the fifty states are either coloured blue (Democratic) or red (Republican) according to the party affiliation of the winning candidate.

boll weevils The collective slang name given to traditional, more conservative **southern Democrats,** who occasionally are at odds with the more liberal, northern wing of the **Democratic Party.** These southern politicians are the direct descendants of a time when the Democratic Party dominated the south of the United States. These conservatives tended to oppose 'big-government' and champion **states' rights**. Indeed, southern Democrats, unwilling to be dictated to by the **federal government,** led the southern states into **secession,** and the **civil war** of the 1860s. Northern Democrats joined with the Republicans in opposing the secession, and abolishing slavery. There has been tension between the two branches of the **Democratic Party** ever since. In particular, during the civil rights era of the 1950s and 1960s, many southern Democrats opposed the desegregation measures advocated by the party's leadership. Boll weevil can be regarded as a pejorative term, as it the name of a pest that destroys the cotton plant.

Boston tea party An incident in 1773 where dissenters dumped chests of tea into Boston harbour. They were protesting at the British government's imposition of a tax on tea in the colonies, and the British East India Company's perceived monopoly on the sale of this commodity. This was a case where the argument that there should be no taxation without representation was used. If the British government was to tax subjects in the colonies, Americans demanded that they should enjoy political representation. The Boston tea party is seen as one of the preliminary acts of the **War of Independence.**

Brady Handgun Violence Prevention Act, 1993 A Congressional act that requires licensed retailers of firearms to conduct background checks on individuals before selling weapons to them. The legislation originally imposed a waiting period of up to five days between applying to purchase a gun and the actual sale. The Brady Act brought these measures to thirty-two states that had previously resisted such degrees of gun control. The success of the Act has been a topic of considerable debate, especially since many guns are acquired in the United States not from licensed dealers but from the 'secondary' market, while the five-day waiting period was replaced by an 'instant' national background check facility in 1998. The bill was named after Jim Brady, former press secretary of **President** Ronald **Reagan**, who was shot and seriously wounded during an assassination attempt on the President in 1981.

bringing home the bacon see **pork barrel politics**

broad construction see **flexible construction**

Brown v. *Board of Education*, **1954** A **Supreme Court** decision that can be regarded as a major milestone in promoting racial equality in the United States. Despite the **civil war** being fought, and **constitutional amendments** enacted almost one hundred years before this case, many southern states still practised legally sanctioned racial discrimination during the 1950s and 1960s. Being asked to judge whether a local education board had the right to provide separate schools for black and white children, the **Supreme Court** ruled that such discrimination was unconstitutional. What is more, the judgment also stated that even if a school board had made provision for both sets of children, ensuring an equal allocation of resources and opportunities (which was not the case), separate provision would still be unconstitutional. As the text of the decision stated, 'separate educational facilities are inherently unequal'. This ruling established a precedent leaving a whole host of discriminatory public services open to legal challenge, and marked the beginning of a (slow) **desegregation** process in the southern states over the next two decades. *Brown* v. *Board of Education* represented the first major victory for the American **civil rights movement**.

Buckley v. *Valeo*, **1976** A **Supreme Court** decision that rendered part of the **Federal Election Campaign Act, 1971**

(FECA) unconstitutional, having deemed the spending of money a form of political expression. FECA had sought to set an upper limit on how much money federal candidates could spend on an election campaign, and to restrict donations from individual citizens and organisations to such campaigns. The **appellants** in this case argued that such restrictions were a violation of **first amendment rights** of free speech, and that the act should be annulled. The *Buckley* v. *Valeo* judgment partially agreed with the appellants. One area where the Court expressed concern over infringements upon the First Amendment was the fact that FECA limited the amount of money a candidate could spend on their own campaign. After the Court gave its **opinion**, candidates were free to spend much as they wanted on their election bid (unless they agreed to accept public funding, and the conditions attached to this). Equally, *Buckley* v. *Valeo* partially invalidated FECA with respect to campaign contributions. Although the judgment supported restrictions on direct donations to campaigns (**hard money**), the Court ruled that US citizens and groups of citizens should not be hindered in spending money on political activities *independent* of these official campaigns. There should be no restrictions on the buying of airtime, for example, to express a view that did not directly advocate the election of a candidate. This opened the way for the use of **soft money** on **issue advertisements**.

Budget and Accounting Act, 1921 An act of Congress that centralised, and made more efficient, the federal budget process. The act requires the **President** to submit to **Congress** a consolidated annual budget proposal and statement on the US government's finances. It also established the **General Accounting Office**, which was charged with auditing the government's accounts. From this point in time, the **executive branch** has taken the lead in setting the **federal government**'s budget, albeit subject to Congressional approval. Previously, budget allocations were determined by various Congressional committees, and were thus potentially too vulnerable to **parochial** political deals struck between legislators.

budget deficit The amount to which a government's spending exceeds its income over a given period. A series of budget deficits from the 1970s onwards saw the **national debt** of the United States rise to record levels during the 1980s and 1990s. As a consequence, this debt became a significant political issue. Several pieces of Congressional legislation have been passed in recent years in an attempt to balance the federal budget, resulting in a number of years of budget surpluses by the start of the twenty-first century. The national debt of the United States, however, still remains at historically high levels. There have been a number of attempts over the last decade to pass a **constitutional amendment** requiring the **executive branch** to maintain a balanced budget.

Budget Enforcement Act, 1990 see **national debt**

Bull Moose Party The nickname of the Progressive Party. This alias derives from the party leader, Theodore Roosevelt, who told reporters that he felt as strong as a 'bull moose' on the occasion of the organisation's inauguration.

Burger Court see **Burger**, Warren

Burger, Warren (1907–95) Having been active in **Republican Party** politics in the state of Minnesota, and served as

President Dwight Eisenhower's Assistant Attorney General, Warren Earl Burger was President Richard Nixon's nominee for Chief Justice of the Supreme Court in 1969. Nixon appointed Burger as a strict constructionist and a person who would exercise judicial restraint. However, the Burger Court did not unleash a counter attack against the decisions of the previous, more liberal, Warren Court, as many predicted. Although the Burger years can be characterised by a degree of conservatism, prominent judgements such as *Roe* v. *Wade,* *1973, United States* v. *Nixon,* 1974 and *Regents of the University of California* v. *Bakke,* 1978 still emerged. Burger retired from the Court in 1986.

Bush, George (1924–) George Herbert Walker Bush was President of the United States between 1989 and 1993. Having made money in the oil industry, Bush started a political career in his home state of Texas, before moving on to serve several Republican Party Presidents in Washington DC. Prior to reaching the White House, he was appointed Ambassador to the United Nations by Richard Nixon, he was Chair of the Republican National Committee, Director of the Central Intelligence Agency, and was elected as Ronald Reagan's Vice President in 1980. Bush's presidency can be categorised as moderately conservative, consolidating many initiatives of the early Reagan administrations. In international affairs, Bush readily used military force to secure US interests abroad, most notably acting to topple the Manuel Noriega regime in Panama during 1989, and leading an international coalition that successfully resisted Saddam Hussein's invasion of Kuwait in 1991. On the domestic front, Bush worked with the Congress to reduce the federal budget deficits, but he failed to get re-elected in 1992 due to popular dissatisfaction with the US economy, which had entered recession. George Bush is the father of George W. **Bush,** who later also became President of the United states.

Bush, George W. (1946–) George Walker Bush assumed the presidency of the United States in January 2001, and was elected for a second term of office in 2004. The son of a former **President,** George **Bush,** Bush junior followed his father into the Texas oil and gas industries after graduating from Yale University, and service in the Air National Guard. Controversy surrounds this period of Bush's life. Conflicting views exist over his military record during the time of the **Vietnam War,** as well as his business dealings. Bush has also stated that he drank too much alcohol during these years. However, having become a born-again Christian, Bush put this period of his life behind him, and again followed in his father's footsteps to become active in Texan politics. He served as **governor** of this state between 1995 and 2000.

In November 2000, Bush was elected President of the United States. Again, this event was surrounded by controversy. In an extremely close poll, Bush actually won fewer popular votes than his opponent Al Gore, but gained the support of more delegates in the **electoral college.** Bush was confirmed President after the **Supreme Court,** in its judgment *Bush* v. *Gore,* 2000, denied Gore the right to a manual recount of votes cast in the state of Florida.

The acts of terrorism in New York City and Washington DC on 11 September 2001 dominated George W. Bush's years in the **White House.** The administration's response, the 'War on Terror', saw the United States lead military invasions of first Afghanistan and then Iraq. Also part of Bush's international agenda was the President's refusal to sign the Kyoto environmental agreement aimed at trying to stem global warming. His administration considered the Kyoto protocols too damaging to US business interests. On the domestic front, the Bush Administration concentrated on implementing tax cuts.

Bush v. *Gore*, 2000 A **Supreme Court** decision that effectively decided the outcome of the 2000 presidential election. The Court's judgment terminated a manual re-count of ballot papers in Florida, resulting in the state assigning its **electoral college** votes to George W. **Bush**, securing this candidate's passage to the **White House**. This contest eventually hung on the ability of machine readers in the state of Florida to efficiently detect **chads** (the hole made in a ballot paper punch card indicating a voter's intention). With the machine count being so tight (Bush beat Gore by just 327 votes) attention turned to the punch cards themselves. It was found that many had not been pierced cleanly (so-called '**hanging chads**') and thus had not been counted correctly. As a result, the Gore camp argued that the result was unsafe, and requested a *manual* count of the ballot cards. Electoral law in the state of Florida, however, required a result to be declared within seven days of the poll. After several court cases contested between the Bush and Gore camps, trying to establish whether Gore had the right to a manual recount or not, the matter arrived at the Supreme Court, which settled the issue in favour of George W. Bush.

C

cabinet The highest committee within the federal **executive branch**, consisting of the **President**, **Vice President** and department heads. A number of non-department heads may also be given 'cabinet-level rank' and invited to attend these meetings. Traditionally, the most powerful cabinet members, after the President and Vice President, have been the **Secretary of State**, Secretary of the Treasury, Secretary of Defense and the **Attorney General**. Unlike the parliamentary systems of Europe, the US cabinet is very much only an advisory panel for the **chief executive**. The President alone is responsible for decision-making, and there is not a 'first amongst equals' understanding. The US **constitution** makes no mention of the cabinet, and its members have no powers independent of those of the President. Indeed, cabinet influence has waned historically. In more recent times, Presidents have also sought advice from alternative committees, such as the **National Security Council**.

Cable Satellite Public Affairs Network see **C-SPAN**

Camp David The official country retreat of the US **President**, located in the Catoctin Mountains of Maryland, seventy miles from the **White House**. This residence is designed to be somewhere where Presidents may work more informally, entertain, or simply relax. Most famously, Camp David hosted the 1978 negotiations brokered by President Jimmy **Carter** where Israel and Egypt agreed a peace deal: the Camp David Accords.

campaign finance Candidates seeking public office in the United States spend enormous amounts of money. In the 2004 presidential race, for example, the contestants between them collected over US$880 million in donations. This money was then spent on employing campaign managers (strategists, pollsters, media consultants, lawyers, and so on), organising political rallies, producing electoral literature, and, most expensive of all, buying air time to broadcast advertisements. The scale of the funding available to a candidate determines the nature and scope of that politician's campaign, and their ability to get their message across to the electorate.

By the 1970s, concern had grown that too much money had become involved in US politics. Organised interests (corporations, unions, and lobby groups, for example) were able to make large donations to candidates, and the fear was that a contender could buy political office, rather than be elected by the people on the strength of their ideas or character. Momentum for campaign finance reform began to build.

The **Federal Election Campaign Act, 1971** was passed by **Congress** requiring candidates to officially disclose from whom they received their larger donations. The act was then amended in 1974 to place a ceiling on how much a candidate could spend on their election, and to limit the sum an individual or organisation could give to any one candidate. This amendment was legally challenged in the case of *Buckley* v. *Valeo*, 1976. The **Supreme Court** supported the disclosure element of the 1971 Act, but ruled that there could be no limit on what candidates could spend on their own campaign. Similarly, although the Court supported a ceiling on direct donations to candidates (**hard money**), it stated that citizens were not to be restricted from supporting political activity where there is no explicit call for a candidate's victory or defeat. This latter argument encouraged large sums of **soft money** to be spent in US politics.

With candidates becoming more sophisticated during the 1980s and 1990s, in the way that they used soft money to assist their campaigns, again pressure grew to reduce the influence of money in US elections. Congress eventually passed the **Bipartisan Campaign Reform Act**, of 2002. This piece of legislation restricted the list of activities that soft money could be spent on, as well as providing a tighter legal definition of what constituted an election advertisement. Previously, candidates' campaigns had benefited considerably from 'issue ads', paid for by soft money, which, although they did not specifically endorse any individual for office, encouraged viewers to make such a choice.

Effectively, the recent history of campaign finance has been a series of reforms trying to limit the influence of money in elections. These reforms have been successful, to a degree, in making campaign contributions transparent, and reducing the potential of rich individuals and organisations simply buying influence, but these aims are still being undermined by candidates' use of soft money.

candidate-centred election Where candidates run for office highlighting their own ideas and character, rather than promoting a party **platform**. Given the weaker influence of political parties in the United States, when compared to European countries, individual candidates are often the focus of elections, rather than national party strategies or manifestos.

Capitol Building The building located on **Capitol Hill**, at the heart of Washington DC, which hosts the US **Congress**. Contained within this building are the chambers of the US **Senate** and **House of Representatives**, and over 500 other rooms that serve this legislature. The Capitol Building, especially its towering dome, has come to symbolise American democracy.

Capitol Hill A low hill on the Potomac River's flood plain that was designed to be at the very heart of Washington DC. The **Capitol Building** sits on top of this hill. Given that this area of Washington DC hosts the US **Congress**

and a number of its administrative buildings, the term Capitol Hill is occasionally used as a synonym for the whole **legislative branch** of the **federal government**.

carpetbaggers Northern politicians who moved south after the **civil war** seeking election. They oversaw the **Republican Party**'s programme of **Reconstruction** in the former confederate states. The term carpetbaggers was coined by disgruntled **southern Democrats**, who were highlighting the fact these politicians had no roots in the communities they sought to serve, but instead had arrived from the north with their possessions contained in the fashionable carpet-fabric bags of the period.

Carter, Jimmy (1924–) James Earl Carter was **President** of the United States, holding office between January 1977 and January 1981. After serving as a naval officer and running his family's farm, Carter entered local politics in Georgia, and was elected **Governor** of this state in 1970. Being a political 'outsider', rather than a Washington DC 'insider', Carter's presidency did much to restore respect in the Office of the President after Richard **Nixon**'s earlier resignation in disgrace. However, Carter's domestic agenda, promoting civil rights and social reform, lacked prominent successes because of a hostile **Congress**, while his foreign policy was hampered when US citizens were taken hostage during Iran's Islamist revolution. The Carter Administration also faced economic conditions of both relatively high inflation and high unemployment. This perceived lack of success paved the way for his defeat by Ronald **Reagan** in the 1980 presidential election. Despite these setbacks, the Carter Administration did facilitate the ground-breaking **Camp David** Accords signed between Israel and Egypt in 1978.

categorical grants Federal funding given to state and local governments, or other organisations, where the use of this money is narrowly defined. Recipients do not have the flexibility of spending associated with **block grants**. It is often the case that recipients have to match a proportion of the funds given. The vast majority of federal aid is issued in the form of categorical grants.

caucus A meeting of members of a legislative body or political party. The US **Congress**, for example, has a number of caucuses (for example, the **Congressional Black Caucus,** Congressional Caucus on Women's Issues, and the Dairy Caucus). These forums provide the opportunity for like-minded legislators to meet regularly to discuss how to promote a particular issue.

   A number of states arrange party caucuses as an alternative to the presidential **primary election** process. Local party activists will meet **precinct** by precinct within the state to choose delegates from amongst themselves to attend the **national party conventions**. Caucuses differ from primary elections in that it is party activists within the state that decide who amongst the challengers should be their party's presidential candidate, rather than holding a public poll, in which the general public can participate.

censure A formal rebuke of an individual or organisation for wrongdoing. **Congress,** for example, may pass a motion of censure against one of its own members or the **President** for inappropriate behaviour.

Central Intelligence Agency An agency of the **federal government** that is charged with gathering, analysing and disseminating intelligence related to US national security. Since it was established in 1947, the CIA has provided the

President, the **National Security Council** and other elements of the US government with information identifying potential threats to the United States. The majority of the agency's work is conducted covertly abroad, but the CIA is also involved in counter-intelligence activities on home soil. The agency is not responsible for gathering criminal intelligence or military intelligence. This is the work of the **Federal Bureau of Investigation** and the Defense Intelligence Agency respectively. In the wake of the terrorist attacks on New York City and Washington DC in 2001, there were criticisms that the US intelligence community was too disparate and lacked coordination. The **Department of Homeland Security** was therefore established in 2002, specifically to counter terrorist and potential terrorist activity in the United States, while a new co-ordinating post of Director of National Intelligence was created two years later. A number of the CIA's previous responsibilities have been transferred to these new agencies.

Website: http://www.cia.gov

certiorari, writ of The order issued by the US **Supreme Court** requiring a lower court to submit details of a case, in order that the Supreme Court can review its judgment. Effectively, a writ of certiorari indicates that the Supreme Court is willing to hear an appeal. The Court receives over 5,000 petitions for such writs annually, but only agrees to hear 5 per cent of these cases. A writ will be issued if four justices vote to hear an appeal (the so-called 'rule of four'). *Certiorare* is the Latin verb 'to be informed'.

chad The hole made in a ballot paper punch card indicating a voter's intention. Chads came to the attention of the world during the 2000 **general election**, when George W.

Bush narrowly beat Al Gore to become **President** of the United States. This contest eventually hung on the ability of machine readers in Florida to efficiently detect chads. With the machine count being so tight (Bush beat Gore by just 327 votes), attention turned to the punch cards themselves. It was found that many had not been pierced cleanly (so-called **hanging chads**) and thus not counted correctly. Consequently, the Gore camp argued that the result was unsafe, and requested a *manual* count of the ballot cards. After a short period of legal wrangling in the lower courts, this request was denied by the US **Supreme Court** in its judgement *Bush* v. *Gore*, 2000.

Chappaquiddick see **Kennedy, Edward**

checks and balances A key underlying principle of the US system of government that prevents too much power accumulating with one individual or agency, thus avoiding tyranny. Checks and balances require different parts of the government to work constructively together. The fact that the **President,** for instance, is **Commander in Chief** of the US military is theoretically balanced by the **constitution** stating that only **Congress** can declare war. Other examples of checks and balances include the requirement that both Congress and the President play a role in appointing **Supreme Court** justices and other federal officials, while amendments to the constitution have to be agreed by both the federal and state governments. Even within individual branches of government one can find internal checks and balances. Legislation does not become law, for example, until it is agreed by both the **House of Representatives** and **Senate,** and even then a bill has to receive the President's approval (unless the **chief executive's veto** is overruled by a two-thirds majority in Congress: another check). In summary, checks and balances guarantee that no one individual or agency of government can act in isolation, with each offering scrutiny over the others' actions.

chief diplomat Reference to the US **President**'s constitutionally defined role requiring this individual to 'make treaties' and 'appoint ambassadors'. Building upon this constitutional foundation, the **chief executive** has always played a prominent role in the foreign affairs of the United States. The President will meet other Heads of State promoting American interests, and represent the US at any collective forum of world leaders. However, the constitution, to preserve the system of **checks and balances,** does require the Congress to ratify any treaties negotiated by the President.

chief executive A title (informal) often given to the **President** of the United States, given that this individual heads the **executive branch** of the **federal government**.

Chief Justice The judge that presides over the **Supreme Court,** and is thus the head of the **judicial branch** of the **federal government.** As well as overseeing the work of the Supreme Court, this individual is also required to officiate the oath at the **President**'s inauguration, and preside over any **impeachment** trial brought against the President or **Vice President.** Despite this person's senior position, the Chief Justice's **opinion** only carries the same weight as his or her fellow Supreme Court justices. Likewise, the Chief Justice is appointed in the same manner as the other justices. When the office becomes vacant, the President is free to nominate an individual either already sitting on the bench of the Supreme Court or another candidate from outside this institution. This nomination will then be considered by the **Senate** in a **confirmation hearing.**

Chief of Staff An individual appointed by the **President** to manage the **White House** Office. This individual is responsible for overseeing the work of presidential assistants and advisors, and managing the President's diary. In several administrations, the Chief of Staff became a very powerful figure, especially as they acted as a 'gatekeeper', deciding who had access to the chief executive. In other administrations, the post held less significance. Indeed, presidents John F. **Kennedy** and Lyndon B. **Johnson** failed to appoint an official Chief of Staff at all, while Jimmy **Carter** only did so towards the end of his term of office.

Christian Right A collective term for conservative political activists in the United States who consider traditional religious values to be at the heart of their political demands. High on the agenda of the Christian Right are a number of social issues, such as opposing abortion, euthanasia, genetic engineering, and gay rights. Many within this movement also wish to see religion play a more prominent role in US schooling, something currently prohibited by the **Supreme Court**'s interpretation of the US **constitution**. The Christian Right, known more commonly as the 'moral majority' at this time, developed as a political force during the 1970s. **President** Ronald **Reagan** received considerable support from this constituency in the 1980s, whilst, more recently, President George W. **Bush** has also been associated with the Christian Right.

Christmas tree bill A legislative bill that has had so many amendments attached to it, it can be likened to a Christmas tree adorned with numerous decorations. Usually considered towards the end of a legislative session, many of the amendments attached involve the allocation of funds that have little relation to the subject of the original bill.

CIA see **Central Intelligence Agency**

Civil Rights Act, 1964 An act of **Congress** that attempted to end discrimination on the basis of race, colour, national origin or religion in the United States. In particular, the act made it illegal to discriminate in public spaces, in the workplace, and schools. The **federal government** considered it had the right to pass this legislation, and impose these conditions on the states, as all these specified categories were involved within the federal jurisdiction of **interstate commerce**. The act also addressed how states granted the franchise to their citizens, and equal employment rights for women.

The 1964 Civil Rights Act was the first major piece of federal legislation to address the issue of **segregation** since the **reconstruction** period after the **civil war**. It came at the height of the **civil rights** campaign seeking to establish equality in the United States for African-Americans. Southern states still opposed integration, and many southern politicians continued to be elected on a segregationist **ticket**. Indeed, after these politicians had failed to block this legislation in the Congress, a legal challenge against the act was launched. In the **Supreme Court** opinion of *Heart of Atlanta Motel* v. *United States, 1964*, however, the Civil Rights Act was upheld.

The 1964 Civil Rights Act, combined with the **Voting Rights Act, 1965**, and the earlier Supreme Court decision of *Brown* v. *Board of Education, 1954*, can be regarded as the three key events in the federal government's attempts to remove segregation from the United States.

civil rights movement A campaign seeking racial desegregation in the southern region of the United States during the

1950s and 1960s, which then went on to address racial discrimination in the whole of the country. Although the **abolitionists** and the **civil war** had brought about the end of slavery in the United States, and civil rights had been granted to all via the Fourteenth and Fifteenth Amendments to the US **constitution**, African-Americans failed to secure equal opportunities for a century after these events. Indeed, in the southern states, state law actively discriminated against the black population. By the 1950s, organisations such as the **National Association for the Advancement of Colored People** and the Southern Christian Leadership Conference were successfully challenging this state of affairs.

Landmark victories for the civil rights movement include: *Brown* v. *Board of Education,* **1954**, with the **Supreme Court** ruling that segregation in schools was unconstitutional; the 1955 **Montgomery bus boycott** in Alabama, which forced this city to integrate its public transport network; President Eisenhower deploying federal troops in 1957 to ensure African-American students could attend **Little Rock Central High School** in Arkansas, defying the state **governor's** efforts to stop this; the **Civil Rights Act, 1964** that effectively enforced desegregation in public places; and the **Voting Rights Act, 1965** that prevented the franchise from being manipulated to deny blacks rights of political representation. Southern state governments resisted all of these actions, and occasionally protests led to violence. A number of civil rights campaigners lost their lives during this period, including most notably the assassinations of leading activists Martin Luther **King** and **Malcolm X**.

Having secured desegregation and a stronger legal foundation to confront discrimination, the civil rights movement since the 1950s and 1960s has been about consolidating these rights through stronger enforcement measures, and tackling the issue of considerable wealth and opportunity gaps that exist between blacks and whites in the United States. **Affirmative action** is seen by many campaigners as a method of addressing these inequalities.

civil war A war, 1861 to 1865, fought between the **federal government** and eleven southern states that seceded from the Union to form their own **Confederate States of America**. Tensions grew between the northern and southern states as their respective economies developed different needs. The north forged ahead with industrialisation and developing a manufacturing base, while the south relied more upon an agrarian economy. Plantations, worked by slave labour, were at the heart of this southern economy. As slavery became a more contentious issue, southern politicians became concerned over calls emanating from the north to restrict this institution in the United States, culminating with the **abolitionists'** campaign to ban slavery altogether. Alongside the issue of slavery was the south's resentment over what was perceived as the federal government's infringement on states' rights (and the 'southern way of life' in general), as well as a national tariff policy that favoured the industrial north over the agrarian south. When the (northern) **Republican Party** administration of Abraham **Lincoln** took office in 1861, eleven southern states judged their interests no longer to be served by the Union, and seceded, forming their own confederacy. The federal government deemed this secession illegal, and a civil war ensued.

The number of casualties suffered in this conflict still outnumbers total combined losses from all other battles in which US troops have been involved, from the **War of Independence**, through the two world wars, to

Vietnam and the Gulf. The Union (federal) army was eventually victorious, served by its superior numbers and resources, which ensured the preservation of the United States, and led to the abolition of slavery (through the **emancipation proclamation** and **Thirteenth Amendment**). A period of **reconstruction** then ensued, to bring the southern states back into the Union.

Clinton, Bill William Jefferson Clinton served two terms as **President** of the United States between 1993 and 2001. From a humble background, Clinton won scholarships and graduated from Georgetown and Oxford universities before entering politics in his home state of Arkansas as a **Democratic Party** candidate. He served as this state's **Attorney General** and then as its **Governor.**

As President, Clinton presided over a period of considerable economic success, where the **federal government** returned surpluses after years of **budget deficit**. A number of social reforms were also successfully enacted. The Clinton years, however, were also characterised by a confrontational relationship between the **executive branch** and the **Congress**. Early on, Congress was to reject Clinton's complex health reform bill, and, then, in Clinton's second term, **Speaker of the House of Representatives** Newt **Gingrich** attempted to push through an alternative, more conservative, legislative programme, termed the **Contract with America**. The relationship between the two branches of government was also soured by Congress authorising a number of investigations addressing Clinton's public and personal conduct. These investigations culminated in the **House of Representatives** impeaching President Clinton on the grounds of 'obstruction of justice'. This charge related to an earlier enquiry questioning the president's relationship with Monica **Lewinsky**, a **White House** intern. Clinton is only the second President to have been impeached in the history of the United States (Andrew Johnson being the first in 1868, and with Richard **Nixon** resigning before **impeachment** charges were heard). As with Andrew Johnson's case, however, a less **partisan Senate** acquitted Clinton of the House charges, and the impeachment process failed.

Clinton v. *the City of New York*, 1998 see **line-item veto**

cloakrooms, Congressional see **Congressional cloakrooms**

closed primary A **primary election** where voters are required to declare a party affiliation, determining which political party's primary process they can participate in.

cloture A rule of the United States **Senate**, introduced in 1917, that permits the ending of debate, and the bringing of a bill to an immediate vote, should three-fifths of members support the call for cloture. Prior to this date, the Senate had no formal mechanism for curtailing the debating stage of a bill. Senators had the right to talk for as long as they wished. This left legislation vulnerable to **filibuster**, where a small minority of members could block the passage of a bill simply by refusing to stop debating on the **floor** of the Senate, until the bill's sponsors withdrew their legislation. The **House of Representatives** has no such cloture rule, as debates in this chamber are assigned time constraints.

Commander in Chief Article One, Section Eight of the US **constitution** assigns the **President** the role of Commander in Chief of the United States military. He or she is responsible for the military's deployment, and assignment of duties. In order to maintain **checks and balances**, although the president commands these forces, only **Congress** may declare war. The **Senate** must also confirm the **chief executive**'s choice of senior officers. Despite being the Commander in Chief, the President is not actually a member of the military. This keeps the armed forces strictly under civilian control.

commerce clause Reference to a sentence in the US **constitution** that requires **Congress** to 'regulate commerce with foreign nations, and among the several states, and with the Indian tribes' (Article One, Section Eight). As well as dealing with international trade, the **Founding Fathers** charged the **federal government** with supervising internal, interstate commerce, due to harmful tariff wars that had developed between the states immediately after the **War of Independence**. Over time, this commerce clause has permitted the federal government to legislate on a broad range of economic and social issues, previously deemed to be within the **jurisdiction** of the states. This is because, as the US economy expanded, nearly all commerce came to involve the crossing of state boundaries. For example, in the middle of the twentieth century, Congress passed legislation to set national minimum labour standards. Although the constitution does not specifically make the federal government the custodian of labour rights, the **Supreme Court,** in the case of *United States* v. *Darby Lumber Company*, 1941 confirmed this legislation to be constitutional. This was because goods produced under sub-standard labour conditions would be transported by interstate commerce. Similarly, the **Civil Rights Act, 1964** was deemed constitutional by the Court in the case of *Heart of Atlanta Motel* v. *United States,* **1964.** In this instance, Congress was allowed to pass legislation prohibiting racial segregation in public places, because a number of customers staying at the Heart of Atlanta motel, travelling sales persons for example, did so in order to enable them to conduct interstate commerce. A broad interpretation of the commerce clause has thus allowed the federal government to introduce legislation setting national social and economic standards.

Committee on Rules see **rules committees**

Committee on Ways and Means see **House of Representatives Committee on Ways and Means**

committee system Given the volume and complexity of **Congress'** responsibilities, much of the **legislative branch**'s work is undertaken at committee level. Members of both the **Senate** and **House of Representatives** divide themselves up into respective committees, and specialise in certain aspects of US government. These committees will scrutinise proposed legislation emanating from the **executive branch**; introduce their own bills; hold hearings involving outside experts to inform themselves about a certain area of policy; hold similar hearings to question executive officials by way of **oversight**; and generally manage this area of legislative responsibility on behalf of the US Congress as a whole. Any legislation that a committee does recommend after its internal deliberations will subsequently be tabled for debate on the Senate or House **floor**, where all members can assess the proposal, and make amendments accordingly. Committees do the specialist work, ensuring efficiency, but it is the responsibility of the whole of Congress to actually pass legislation. Examples of the most prestigious committees on which members of Congress seek membership are the Senate Foreign Relations Committee, the **House of Representatives**

Rules Committee, and the **House of Representatives Ways and Means Committee.**

compound republic A phrase used by James **Madison** to describe the representative, federal, political system constructed by the US **constitution**. In particular, 'compound republic' refers to the partnership between the states and the central government who have separate sovereign powers, but also act as a **check and balance** upon each other.

concurrent powers Powers shared between two or more governments. The US **constitution** determines that, although the federal and state governments have sovereign **jurisdiction** where they govern separately, other tasks are shared. In the case of road transportation, for example, both levels of government are involved in building an integrated national road system. Other concurrent powers include raising taxes and establishing law courts.

concurring opinion see **opinion of the Supreme Court**

Confederate States of America The group of eleven southern states that attempted to secede from the United States in 1860–1, sparking the **civil war.** The states of South Carolina, Mississippi, Florida, Alabama, Georgia, Louisiana, Texas, Virginia, Arkansas, Tennessee, and North Carolina considered their interests no longer served by the **federal government,** particularly in light of the north's hostility towards slavery and a tariff policy that favoured northern manufacturing industry over southern agriculture. The seceding states argued that states' rights had been abused. The federal government deemed the secession illegal, and a civil war ensued. Although strong enough to fight for four years, eventually the Confederacy was overwhelmed by superior numbers and resources. After General Robert Lee surrendered the Confederate army at Appomattox, Virginia, in 1865, the Confederate States of America soon collapsed and this territory reunited with the rest of the United States after a period of **reconstruction**.

confederation A loose political union of states. Confederal cooperation involves members ceding less sovereignty, and forming a weaker central power, than required under a federal system.

conferees Members of **Congress** assigned respectively by the **Senate** and **House of Representatives** to act for these bodies in a **conference committee**.

conference committee In order for a bill to be passed by the US **Congress**, its provisions need to be approved by both the **Senate** and the **House of Representatives**. This requires an identical piece of legislation, word for word, to be agreed by the two chambers. Due to different amendments placed on bills during their respective passages through the Senate and the House, or even as a result of different starting proposals, legislation rarely attains the uniformity required. This is where the conference committee comes into play. **Conferees** are delegated by the two chambers to negotiate a compromise bill, harmonising the Senate's and the House's proposals. A report of the newly unified bill is then sent back by the conference committee to both **floors** of the Congress, for final approval.

Conference of Mayors see **United States Conference of Mayors**

confirmation hearing As part of the **checks and balances** system, the US **constitution** requires presidential appointments to be approved by the **Senate**. In order to assess these nominees, the Senate holds confirmation hearings. Cabinet members, judges, military officers, ambassadors and other high-ranking **executive branch** officials are questioned by assigned Senate committees, and a judgment made on the nominee's competence and character. On the whole, **partisan** politics are avoided, given the **President**'s constitutional right to staff the **executive branch**. Less than a dozen cabinet nominees have been rejected by these hearings since 1789. Thirty other candidates have failed to be approved (either formally in a vote, or the nomination being withdrawn by the President). One of Ronald **Reagan**'s **Supreme Court** choices, Robert Bork, for example, was rejected because his conservative views were unacceptable to Senators close to women's and minority group interests, while one of Richard **Nixon**'s Court nominations, Clement Haynsworth, failed to gain office because of Senate doubts over this person's ability to do the job.

Congress The US Congress is the **legislative branch** of the **federal government**. It was initially convened in New York City, and met in Philadelphia, before finding a permanent home in the US **Capitol Building, Washington DC**, since 1800. Congress is the collective name for the two chambers, the **Senate** and the **House of Representatives**, that together have the sole responsibility for making US federal law (subject to presidential assent). Each state elects two candidates to serve in the Senate, regardless of its population size, while constituencies of the House of Representatives reflect demographics, with larger states sending more Representatives to Congress than less populous ones. Both the Senate and House have

to approve a bill before it is sent to the **President** for enact-
ment. The US **constitution** defines the areas in which
Congress is permitted to make law: namely the power to
collect taxes, borrow money on behalf of the United
States, regulate commerce, coin money, declare war, raise
and support armies, and make all laws necessary and
proper for the execution of its powers. The so-called **commerce clause** and **necessary and proper clause** have been
interpreted broadly to permit Congress to expand its legislative role alongside the development of the United
States itself as a modern industrial state.

Alongside its legislative role, Congress, by way of
checks and balances, also has an **oversight role** with
respect to the other branches of government. Overseeing
the **executive branch**, for example, senior presidential
appointments have to be confirmed by the Senate, and
Congressional hearings will be regularly held investigating the executive's proposed legislation and the manner
in which laws are implemented.

The term 'Congress' is also used to refer to the two-
year periods between federal **general elections** (itself
divided into two annual sessions). George **Washington**
was therefore President at the time of the first Congress,
while George W. **Bush**'s second term of office commenced
with the first session of the 109th Congress.

Website: http://www.house.gov or http://www.Senate.
gov

Congress of the Confederation The title of the national government that served the United States between 1781 and
1789, under the **Articles of Confederation**. This body was
the successor to the **Continental Congress**, which had successfully prosecuted the **War of Independence**, and was
superseded by the US **Congress** on ratification of the
current **constitution**. The Congress of the Confederation

should not be confused with the government of the **Confederate States of America,** which governed the break-away southern states during the **civil war** period of the mid-nineteenth century.

Congressional Black Caucus A loose association of African-American Congressional members, operating since 1969, who cooperate to address the legislative interests of black and minority citizens. Over the years, the Caucus has been involved with issues such as promoting welfare reform and inner city regeneration, advocating sanctions against apartheid South Africa, and attempting to expand educational opportunities.

Website: http://www.congressionalblackcaucus.net

Congressional Budget and Impoundment Control Act, 1974 see **Congressional Budget Office**

Congressional Budget Office (CBO) An advisory and research agency assisting **Congress** in its economic and budgetary legislation. This office was established by the Congressional Budget and Impoundment Control Act, 1974 in an effort to counter the **President**'s perceived advantage over Congress in recommending the annual federal budget. After the CBO's formation, Congress was now in a position to scrutinise the president's proposals more closely, using a level of expertise and recourses previously only enjoyed by the **executive branch**. The establishment of the CBO was one of several measures Congress took in the wake of the **Watergate** scandal enabling the **legislative branch** to offer more scrutiny over the executive.

Website: http://www.cbo.gov

Congressional cloakrooms Rooms adjacent to the legislative chambers of the **Senate** and **House of Representatives**

in the **Capitol Building,** originally used by members of **Congress** to hang their hats and overcoats. Today, these rooms provide informal meeting spaces where Representatives and Senators can discuss legislative deals and strategy.

Congressional committees see **committee system**

Congressional hearings Where **Senate** and **House of Representatives** committees and sub-committees hear testimony from **executive branch** officials or outside experts. This evidence helps Congress inform its legislative and **oversight** duties. Before passing a bill that imposes economic sanctions on a foreign government, for example, the Senate Committee on Foreign Relations will seek the opinions of high-ranking executive officials, in the **State Department** say, as well as collecting advice from those outside government (academics, corporate representatives, interest groups, and so on). Likewise, by way of oversight, this Committee will later question executive officials over the implementation of this sanctions legislation. Parallel hearings will take place in the House.

Other examples of oversight hearings include investigations into the official and personal conduct of government officials. When allegations arose over **President** Richard **Nixon**'s role in the **Watergate** scandal, for instance, the Senate created a Select Committee on Presidential Campaign Activities. This body heard testimonies from the President's staff, and the evidence collected eventually led Congress to start **impeachment** hearings against Nixon.

Connecticut Compromise The 1787 settlement negotiated by the **Founding Fathers** at the Philadelphia constitutional convention balancing the level of political representation enjoyed by large and small states within the US **Congress**. Initially, the smaller states at the convention had favoured each state having an equal number of members in Congress, while larger states desired levels of representation in proportion to a state's total population. The 'Connecticut', or 'Great', compromise established a **bi-cameral legislature,** where the **Senate** would have two members from each state whatever this state's demography, while the **House of Representatives** would comprise constituencies taking into account the size of a state's population. The Connecticut compromise also decreed that any bill addressing the raising of money should originate in the House, and that slaves and taxed Indians should be counted as three-fifths of a US citizen when calculating the size of the House of Representatives' constituencies. This agreement is known as the Connecticut Compromise as it was first proposed by delegates from this state.

constitution The supreme law of the United States which defines this country's federal institutions, and the internal relationships between these institutions. The constitution also dictates the association between federal and state governments, and outlines the political rights of US citizens.

Written during the summer of 1787, at a Philadelphia convention of fifty-five delegates (the so-called **Founding Fathers**), the constitution revolves around three interlinked principles: a **separation of the powers, checks and balances,** and **limited government**. In terms of a separation of the powers, there are three branches of the federal government: a **legislative branch,** an **executive branch** and a **judicial branch.** Power is further divided by the fact that the federal and state governments govern separate sovereign **jurisdictions**. This is designed to prevent any one individual or institution becoming too powerful. The separation of powers is reinforced by in-built checks and balances. Each branch of government relies on the cooperation of others to perform its duties. The **President** of the United States commands the US military, for example, but only **Congress** can declare war. The **chief executive** nominates judges to serve the **Supreme Court,** but the **Senate** must confirm these nominations. Similarly, both the federal and state governments have to agree before the constitution can be amended. Added to this separation of powers and checks and balances is the notion of limited government. The constitution outlines citizens' rights which no political authority is permitted to legislate away.

Article One of the constitution outlines the role of the federal legislative branch: the Congress. Power is divided between a Senate and a **House of Representatives,** and the jurisdiction in which they can make laws is clearly defined (the right to levy taxes, borrow money, regulate interstate commerce, provide for military forces, and declare war, amongst others). The Congress also exercises **oversight** powers with respect to the other branches of government, including the right to impeach the President for 'high crimes and misdemeanours'.

Article Two vests the executive power of the United States in one individual: the President. This person is charged with overseeing the implementation of federal law, and is **Commander in Chief** of the US military, and represents the United States in foreign affairs through appointing ambassadors and negotiating treaties (both subject to Senate confirmation).

Article Three places the judicial power of the United States in a Supreme Court. This section of the constitution guarantees that the justices serving this institution are protected from political pressure in that they cannot be removed from post provided they serve with 'good behaviour', nor can their salary be reduced whilst in office.

Article Four concerns itself with the relations between states (the extradition of citizens accused of crimes across state boundaries, for example), and the relationship between the federal government and the states (the federal government is required to guarantee the military security of the individual states).

Article Five outlines the process for amending the constitution. This is executed via cooperation between the Congress and state legislatures.

Article Six ensures that the new government is liable for debts incurred by the previous administration under the **Articles of Confederation**. It also makes plain that the constitution is the supreme law of the United States.

Article Seven determined the ratification procedure for the document, a process which was completed by the states by 1791.

Since ratification, there have been twenty-seven **constitutional amendments**. These changes to the original document have allowed the constitution to evolve alongside US society itself. Individual liberties were defined in the first ten amendments, collectively known as the **Bill of Rights**. Other amendments have addressed the franchise in the United States, slowly proceeding towards a situation where all adults have the right to vote and can directly elect their political representatives. The end of slavery was confirmed by a constitutional amendment, as was the guarantee of constitutional protection for all US citizens (including the ex-slaves). Likewise, there have been administrative clarifications: for instance, defining the succession of administrations, and of the **Vice President** to the office of the President, should the incumbent be incapacitated. A constitutional amendment also prevents any one individual being elected more than twice as President of the United States.

The constitution, however, has not evolved only via formal amendments. Each generation interprets this document in its own way, in order to ensure the constitution's continued relevance as society progresses. Supreme Court interpretations of the **necessary and proper clause**, alongside the **commerce clause**, for example, have allowed Congress to legislate in areas of society and the economy not envisaged by the Founding Fathers. Indeed, the Supreme Court itself has taken on this role of judging what is, and is not, constitutional (known as **judicial review**) via just such an informal amendment: the case of *Marbury* v. *Madison*, 1803. It is to the credit of the original document, and the relevance of these subsequent amendments, both formal and informal, that the constitution is still so revered and respected by US citizens today.

constitutional amendments Thomas **Jefferson** considered that a **constitution**, like the Earth itself, belongs to 'the living, and not the dead'. No constitution should bind future generations to outdated forms of governing. Consequently, the **Founding Fathers** imbedded within the US constitution a mechanism enabling this document to be amended. Should two-thirds of both houses of **Congress** agree to a change, the proposed amendment is sent to the state legislatures, three-quarters of which must agree with this revision for it to be **ratified**. An alternative process permitted by the constitution, as yet unused, is a constitutional convention to be called by Congress at the request of two-thirds of the states. This convention's proposed amendments are then required to be ratified by three-quarters of the state legislatures or, alternatively, by three-quarters of specially convened state constitutional conventions. There have been twenty-seven successful constitutional amendments since 1789.

Amendments to the US constitution can usefully be categorised into five groups: those protecting individual rights; those expanding the franchise; those dealing with the aftermath of slavery and the **civil war**; procedural clarifications; and miscellaneous items.

The first ten amendments to the constitution, approved in 1791, soon after the ratification of the original document itself, are collectively known as the **Bill of Rights**. These address individual liberties. A number of the states only agreed to ratify the original constitution after assurances that this Bill of Rights would soon follow. These first ten amendments guarantee that the freedom of speech, association and worship of US citizens cannot be legislated away by government. Similarly, they entitle any individual accused of a crime to the due process of law (those detained must be charged and tried, have a right to legal representation, a right to silence, and no 'cruel or unnatural punishments' administered for those found guilty, amongst other provisions). The Bill of Rights also protects citizens from having soldiers billeted upon them without consent, and gives individuals the right to form militias and own weapons in order to protect national security.

As well as to conserve individual liberty, constitutional amendments have also been used to expand the franchise in the United States. The Seventeenth Amendment (1913) provided for the direct election of senators, with the people deciding themselves, rather than the state legislatures, who would represent the state in Washington DC. The Nineteenth Amendment (1920) guaranteed the voting rights of women. The Twenty-third Amendment (1961) gave the residents of the **District of Columbia** the right to vote in presidential elections. The Twenty-sixth Amendment (1971) guaranteed that individuals eighteen years old or over could not be denied the vote on account of their age.

The conclusion of the **civil war**, and subsequent efforts to extend equal rights to ex-slaves and the descendents of slaves, also prompted a number of constitutional amendments. The **Thirteenth Amendment** (1865) prohibits slavery in the United States. The Fourteenth Amendment (1868) defined US citizenship in such a way as to include ex-slaves. The Fifteenth Amendment (1870) bars federal and state governments from denying any citizen the right to vote on the grounds of race, colour or previous enslavement. Over ninety years later, with the descendents of ex-slaves still being discriminated against, the Twenty-fourth Amendment (1964) was ratified, which prohibits state governments from denying citizens the right to vote should they not be able to afford a poll tax.

A number of constitutional amendments have been ratified in order to better define the procedures of government in the United States. The **Twelfth Amendment** (1804) clarified how the US **President** and **Vice President** are elected. The Twentieth Amendment (1933) delimits precisely the terms of office of the President, Vice President and senators (until noon, 20 January after an election in the case of the former two posts, and noon, 3 January for the senators). This measure also clarifies the succession process between administrations. The **Twenty-second Amendment** (1951) prevents any individual being elected President more than two times, a response to **Franklin D. Roosevelt** being voted to this post four times, while the **Twenty-fifth Amendment** defines the conditions of succession should a President become incapacitated.

The remaining constitutional amendments respectively prevent US citizens and foreigners from suing a state in a federal court, without the consent of that state (Eleventh Amendment, 1795); authorise the federal government to raise a national income tax (Sixteenth Amendment, 1913); ban and reinstate the prohibition of intoxicating liquors in the United States (Eighteenth Amendment of 1919 and Twenty-first Amendment of 1933); and determine that any pay rise the **legislative branch** awards itself will only come into effect after the commencement of the next Congress (Twenty-seventh Amendment of 1992).

The constitution, however, has not evolved solely via formal amendments. Each generation interprets this document in its own way, to ensure the constitution's continued relevance as society progresses. **Supreme Court** interpretations of the **necessary and proper clause**, alongside the **commerce clause**, for example, have allowed Congress to legislate in areas of society and the economy not envisaged by the Founding Fathers. Whether it be through formal or informal amendments, the constitution seeks to be a living document.

construction see **strict construction**

Continental Congress The title of the assembly of representatives from the thirteen colonies that met from 1774 onwards in order to make decisions over how to protect American interests under British rule. This body subsequently provided the political leadership behind the prosecution of the **War of Independence**. It was the Continental Congress that appointed George **Washington** to lead the American forces in 1775, and which adopted the **Declaration of Independence** in 1776. After victory against the British, this assembly drew up the **Articles of Confederation**. On the ratification of these Articles in 1781, the Continental Congress was superseded by the **Congress of the Confederation**, which itself gave way to today's US **Congress**, when the current **constitution** was ratified in 1789.

Contract with America As part of the election campaign of 1994, **Republican Party** candidates for the **House of Representatives** signed a 'Contract with America'. Should they be elected, these representatives pledged to undertake a conservative legislative programme that would create, amongst other provisions: a balanced budget **constitutional amendment**, a **line-item veto** to control federal spending, tough anti-crime legislation, welfare reform, reduced federal regulation, and new term limits for politicians. Rarely has a Congressional election been fought on such a defined, national agenda. The Republican Party, partly as a response to this pledge, performed well in this poll. Supporters optimistically called this a 'Republican revolution'.

The Contract was part of a strategy, led by the **Speaker of the House of Representatives**, Newt Gingrich, to counter **President** Bill **Clinton**'s own legislative programme. It was a time of highly partisan politics, with only limited cooperation between the Congress and the **executive branch**. Most of the provisions of the Contract were passed by the House of Representatives, as promised, but several of these items failed to be approved by the **Senate**, or were diluted by it. Republicans in the Senate had not campaigned on this platform.

conventions see **national party conventions**

cooperative federalism A style of **federalism** where national and state institutions govern together in partnership, as opposed to **dual federalism,** where each division of government only concerns itself with its own distinct and separate jurisdiction. Nineteenth-century politics in the United States can be characterised as being akin to dual federalism, while **President** Franklin D. **Roosevelt**'s **New**

Deal is often cited as prompting a new era of cooperative federalism. Seeking economic recovery, state governments willingly worked with the federal government, receiving federal funds and supporting federal initiatives in policy areas that had traditionally been regarded as being solely within the state jurisdiction. Cooperative federalism is sometimes termed **picket-fence federalism** or **marble-cake federalism**.

court-packing Faced with a conservative **Supreme Court** during the 1930s, which had struck down several policies of his **New Deal** on the grounds that these acts were unconstitutional, **President** Franklin D. **Roosevelt** threatened to 'pack' the Court. In order to create a pro-New Deal majority amongst the Supreme Court justices, Roosevelt suggested he would appoint new members to the Court. Although the **constitution** does not allow the President to remove justices once they have been appointed, it does not specifically state how many Supreme Court justices there should be. Roosevelt was threatening to exploit this loophole to install new justices more sympathetic to his legislative programme. Congress rejected this plan on the grounds that it endangered the **separation of the powers** found at the heart of the US constitution. The Supreme Court did, however, review its opposition to the New Deal in the wake of this challenge. It was to be less obstructive to the President's plans from this point on.

creative federalism Where the US **federal government** intervenes directly in political jurisdictions traditionally associated with the states. The federal government is thus interpreting the **constitution** 'creatively' in order to set national standards. The phrase if often associated with **President** Lyndon B. **Johnson,** who attempted to implement legislation during the 1960s addressing **civil rights** and instigating welfare reforms. With the states taking federal money to pay for Johnson's programmes, and abiding by federal guidelines, a new type of federal relationship developed where Washington DC became the senior partner. This type of relationship moved away from the earlier periods of **dual federalism,** where the federal and state governments operated in separate jurisdictions, and **cooperative federalism,** where the two levels of government interlinked their work to a greater degree, but more as equals. Under creative federalism, this equality and cooperation is skewed in favour of federal leadership.

C-SPAN The television company that broadcasts the proceedings of **Congress.** Television cameras were first allowed to cover **floor** debates of the **House of Representatives** in 1979, and of the **Senate** in 1986. C-SPAN also broadcasts **Congressional hearings.** C-SPAN is an abbreviation of Cable Satellite Public Affairs Network.
Website: http://www.c-span.org

Cuban missile crisis A confrontation between the United States and the Soviet Union during 1962, which threatened to escalate into all-out nuclear war. The administration of **President J. F. Kennedy,** after it had supported a failed invasion of Cuba by Cuban exiles in the previous year, had to contend with a Soviet build up of military force in this country. Moscow deployed missile batteries, and considerable numbers of the Red Army. Kennedy responded by blockading Cuba, and drawing up new offensive invasion plans. After a nervous period of stand-off, the Soviet Union agreed to withdraw its missiles and a number of its troops from Cuba, after a pledge from the United States that it would not invade its Caribbean neighbour. Less publicly, but undoubtedly part of the negotiations, US missiles were reciprocally removed from Turkish territory.

D

DC see **District of Columbia**

Declaration of Independence A document, largely penned by Thomas **Jefferson**, and adopted by the **Continental Congress** in 1776, that outlines why the American colonies no longer accepted British rule. With the adoption of this document, hope of addressing the colonists' grievances within the colonial system was at an end. Independence was now the demand, and would be fought for. The text of the Declaration outlines the moral obligations of governments towards their subjects (that power must be a product of the 'consent of the governed', for example, with individuals entitled to 'inalienable rights'), and then goes on to list specific cases where the government of King George III had failed to meet these obligations. These grievances justify and compel the American colonies to fight for their independence, the text argued. The date that the Declaration came into effect, the 4th of July, has become known as Independence Day, and is an annual national holiday in the United States.

delegated powers Those powers granted to the US **Congress** by the **constitution**. In forming a federal government, the states delegated to the national legislature specific areas of sovereign responsibility. These areas are

defined in Article One, Section Eight of the US constitution: namely to manage the national debt; to regulate
commerce between the states, with foreign powers and
the Indian nations; to mint a national currency and
standardise weights and measures; to establish a mail
service and construct roads; to enforce patents and
copyright; to constitute federal courts under the
Supreme Court; to manage the nation's military capability and defend its interests in foreign affairs; to guarantee the internal security of the United States; and
'to make laws which shall be necessary and proper for
carrying into execution the foregoing powers'. Over
time, the scope and reach of Congress' legislation has
grown immensely. The federal government involves
itself in most areas of US society in the twenty-first
century. Yet, every act of Congress must, in some way,
be constitutionally justified by referring back to one of
these delegated powers. In the majority of cases, this has
been helped by a broad interpretation of the **commerce
clause** and the **necessary and proper clause**. The delegated powers are also known as the 'enumerated
powers'.

delegates to the House of Representatives In addition to 435
members serving the state constituencies of the **House of
Representatives**, 4 delegates also sit in this legislative
chamber, along with the Resident Commissioner of
Puerto Rico. These individuals represent the non-state
territories of the United States. Delegates are currently
elected from American Samoa, the District of Columbia,
Guam, and the Virgin Islands. Delegates may participate
in all the House's legislative business, apart from the final
floor vote of any bill. Delegates are elected for two years
at a time, while the Resident Commissioner of Puerto
Rico serves a four-year term.

Democratic National Committee Operating since 1848, the Democratic National Committee (DNC) is the central, national, organisational body of the **Democratic Party**. This committee helps co-ordinate the work of local, state and national Democratic Party organisations and politicians, and promotes the election of its candidates via technical and financial support. In addition, the DNC oversees the quadrennial **national party convention**, and the associated nomination of a Democratic presidential candidate.

Website: http://www.democrats.org

Democratic national convention see **national party convention**

Democratic Party One of the two major political parties found in the United States today. The Democratic Party can trace its origins back to a Congressional **caucus** founded in 1792 by Thomas **Jefferson**, but the party only began to use its modern name, and develop its current institutions, in the 1830s, under the presidency of Andrew **Jackson**. Prior to the 1860s and the **civil war**, the Democrats were the dominant force in US politics. The party championed rural, agrarian interests, and was consistently re-elected to power. This dominance came to an end, however, when the issue of slavery split the party. **Southern Democrats** staunchly sought to preserve this institution, where as slavery enjoyed less support from those in the north. It eventually took the fighting of the civil war to settle this matter.

After the civil war, in terms of national politics, the **Republican Party** prospered at the Democrat's expense. Between 1860 and 1912, the Democrats only won the **White House** twice. The party suffered from being associated with the failed **Confederation of American States**, and by championing rural interests at a time when America's industrial strength was growing. This failure at the presidential level, however, was tempered by the

Democratic Party's continued electoral success in the southern states. Still united by the experience of the civil war, the south consistently voted Democrat.

In the twentieth century, the Democratic Party became a national political force once again. Following Woodrow **Wilson**'s two terms as President (1913–21), the Democrats enjoyed a longer period of dominance starting with the **Great Depression** of the 1930s. This social and economic crisis brought Franklin D. **Roosevelt** to the White House and his **New Deal**. The so-called **New Deal coalition** was built upon the Democrat Party's traditional southern platform, adding to it the support of labour interests, and the African-American vote. This provided a more radical edge to the Democratic Party. Government intervention would now be considered in order to provide welfare reforms targeting disadvantaged sections of society. Similarly, policy was created to protect the civil rights of those discriminated against. Roosevelt's New Deal was followed in the 1960s by J. F. **Kennedy**'s and Lyndon B. **Johnson**'s civil rights legislation, as well as the **Great Society** welfare programme.

Due to the reforms made possible by the New Deal coalition, today the Democratic Party is often associated with labour movements, left-leaning intellectuals, civil rights campaigners, minority groups and women's interests. It would be wrong, however, to compare this party to social democratic movements found in Europe. The Democratic Party still operates within the traditional conservative ideological outlook of the United States, demanding limited government, promotion of the individual, and respect for capitalism. It is an organisation that should be classified as right of centre. Similarly, there remain considerable numbers of socially conservative southern Democrats at the heart of the party, dulling this organisation's radical edge.

Having enjoyed long periods of Congressional and presidential power in the twentieth century, today the Democratic Party faces greater competition from the Republican Party. With the party re-alignment of the last four decades, many southern Democrats have defected to the Republicans. With this break-up of the New Deal coalition, Republican Party candidates have once again been winning the White House, and the Democrats are more regularly losing their majorities in both chambers of Congress.

Website: http://www.democrats.org

denied powers Those powers, outlined by the US **constitution,** that remain in possession of citizens, which cannot be legislated away by the states or the federal government. Provisions contained within the **Bill of Rights,** freedom of speech for example, are denied powers.

Department of Homeland Security A **cabinet** department of the **federal government** established in the wake of the terrorist attacks on New York City and Washington DC in 2001. The department's three aims are to: prevent terrorist attacks within the United States; reduce America's vulnerability to terrorism; and minimise the damage from potential attacks and natural disasters. A number of existing federal agencies, such as the Coast Guard, the Federal Emergency Management Agency, and the Citizenship and Immigration Service, were put under the Department of Homeland Security's control in order to help co-ordinate the counter-terrorism campaign.

Website: http://www.dhs.gov/dhspublic/index.jsp

Department of State The **cabinet** department of the **federal government** charged with managing the foreign affairs of the United States.

Website: http://www.state.gov

Department of the Treasury Created during the first session of Congress in 1789, this **cabinet** department of the **federal government** oversees the finances of the United States. Amongst its roles are collecting federal taxes (via its **Internal Revenue Service** agency), supervising the **national debt**, advising the **President** on financial performance and policy, regulating US banks, and producing the nation's bank notes, coins and postage stamps.

Website: http://www.treasury.gov

desegregation The process of integrating a society, ending the enforced separation of (racial) groups. Despite **constitutional amendments** following the end of the **civil war** that gave African-Americans equal political rights, segregation remained a feature of US society, particularly in the southern states. Many black and white Americans lived apart and used separate public amenities. This was the case until the second half of the twentieth century. States, reluctant to see the end of segregation, took heart from the **Supreme Court** decision of *Plessey* v. *Ferguson*, 1896. This ruling stated that the segregation of public facilities may remain, as long as there was an equal provision between the groups, required under the Fourteenth Amendment: 'Separate but equal' became the justification for discrimination in the south. In reality, African-Americans rarely received equal resources from their governments, and were habitually discriminated against. This situation began to change with the advent of the **civil rights movement**. Responding to an altering social environment, steps were taken initially in the US military to remove racial barriers. Similarly, the Supreme Court, with *Brown* v. *Board of Education*, 1954, effectively reversed *Plessey* v. *Ferguson*. Public services could no longer be segregated. Later, in the 1960s, federal legislation was enacted (**Civil Rights Act, 1964** and **Voting Rights Act, 1965**) attempting to eradicate segregation from the franchise. Despite considerable resistance to these measures from southern state governments, racial barriers began to dissolve.

direct primary A **primary election** where, at the **national party convention,** the victorious delegate is bound to vote for the candidate he or she pledged to support whilst campaigning for the primary. In an indirect primary, the delegate is under no such obligation, and may use their discretion in selecting who to vote for as the party's candidate.

discharging a bill Should a committee of **Congress** refuse to report a bill out of its jurisdiction, and on to the **floor** of the **Senate** or **House of Representatives,** that chamber can vote on a motion of discharge. If a majority vote is received, the bill will proceed to the floor of the chamber for scrutiny in the normal manner, overriding the resistance of the committee.

dissenting opinion If justices of the **Supreme Court** disagree with the majority **opinion** in any case, they may collectively or individually write a dissenting opinion. This document puts into the public domain any arguments against the Court's majority (and prevailing) ruling.

District of Columbia (DC) A tract of land on the Potomac River, ceded to the **federal government** by the state of Maryland. This territory is the location of Washington DC, the US federal capital since 1790. It is home to the **White House,** the **Capitol Building,** the **Supreme Court,** and is the headquarters of the national government. The fact that the core of the federal government is not housed in any of the fifty states, but on separate federal territory, helps reinforce the **division of powers.** Somewhat ironically, precisely because this territory is not a state, residents of DC receive less political representation than other US citizens. Although a constitutional amendment of 1961 let them participate in presidential elections, these residents have no senator, and can only vote for a **delegate to the House of Representatives.** The US **Congress** itself administers the territory. The District is named after Christopher Columbus, the explorer who 'discovered' the Americas in 1492.

divided government see **separation of the powers**

division of powers see **separation of the powers**

Dixiecrat see **southern Democrats**

DNC see **Democratic National Committee**

double jeopardy Being tried for the same crime twice. In order to prevent citizens being harassed by the state, and tried until the prosecution is satisfied, double jeopardy is prevented in the United States by the Fifth Amendment to the US **constitution.** This amendment also prevents individuals being punished for the same crime more than once.

***Dred Scott* v. *Sandford*, 1857** A **Supreme Court** ruling that reinforced the institution of slavery in the United States, and declared the **Missouri Compromise** unconstitutional. Dred Scott, a slave, had been taken to Illinois and the Wisconsin Territory by his master, John **Sandford,** before returning to Missouri. While, at the time, Missouri was a slave state, both Illinois and the

Wisconsin Territory outlawed slavery. Scott therefore sued his master for his liberty, on the premise that he had become a free person once he had entered Illinois. The Supreme Court found against Scott on several counts. In the first instance, the **opinion** ruled that as Scott was a slave, he was not a citizen of the United States, and was not entitled to sue in a federal court. Secondly, the Court decided that Scott had lost any rights he may have had under Illinois law when he returned to Missouri. And finally, the justices declared that Scott was not protected by the Missouri Compromise, where it was possible to hold slaves in western territories below the 36th parallel, but not above it. The Court ruled this act of **Congress** to be unconstitutional as it deprived Sandford of his **Fifth Amendment** rights: property (a slave, in this case) cannot be confiscated without 'due process of law' and 'just compensation'. This was only the second time that the Supreme Court had invalidated an act of Congress.

With this ruling opening the possibility that every citizen was now able to keep slaves, wherever they resided in the United States, tensions between north and south increased. The civil war would begin four years later. The Thirteenth (1865) and Fourteenth (1868) Amendments would finally settle the constitutional nature of slavery in the United States, not *Dred Scott* v. *Sandford*. These changes respectively made keeping slaves illegal nationwide, and granted ex-slaves rights of citizenship.

dual federalism A style of federalism where the central authority and the states govern in separate sovereign areas. Dual federalism is the type of federal/state relationship envisaged by the **Founding Fathers** when they wrote the US **constitution**. This document clearly outlines the duties of the federal government (the so-called **delegated powers**), leaving all other responsibility in the jurisdiction of the states. Thus, power is divided. No one government within the system should encroach on the sovereignty of another. As the twentieth century progressed, however, dual sovereignty became somewhat diluted. The federal government, in an era of so-called **cooperative federalism** and **creative federalism**, could frequently be found operating in policy areas traditionally associated with the states.

due process of law The process that dictates that the state must act fairly and in accordance with established procedures before it punishes a citizen for breaking a law. This punishment must be consummate with the crime committed. US citizens therefore have the right, amongst others, to a fair trial, legal representation, the right to silence, no unwarranted seizure of personal property, and may only be tried once for the same crime. Due process of law is guaranteed by the **Bill of Rights** and the Fourteenth Amendment to the US **constitution**.

E

Eisenhower, Dwight D. (1890–1969) **President** of the United States between 1953 and 1961. Dwight David Eisenhower was a career soldier who rose through the ranks to command the allied forces in Europe during the Second World War. After serving as President Harry **Truman**'s Army Chief of Staff, he became Supreme Commander of the North Atlantic Treaty Organization (NATO) in 1950. Regarded by many Americans as a hero, due to his war record, Eisenhower stood successfully as

the **Republican Party**'s presidential candidate in 1952.
The degree of his popularity can be measured by the fact
that he had earlier also been offered the **Democratic
Party**'s nomination.

Eisenhower's two terms of office were dominated by
foreign affairs, particularly prosecuting the Cold War
against the Soviet Union. He honoured his campaign
pledge to end the **Korean War**, established a number of
security pacts with other nations, sanctioned the **Central
Intelligence Agency** to remove the anti-American governments in Iran and Guatemala, bolstered the Lebanese
government by deploying US marines, and provided
France with assistance (but not troops) in its war against
communist insurgents in Vietnam. In domestic affairs,
Eisenhower largely deferred to the will of **Congress**.
He did, however, initiate the building of the country's
interstate highway network, establish the National Aeronautics and Space Administration (NASA), and help
enforce **desegregation** by deploying federal troops in
1957 to ensure African-American children could attend
Little Rock Central High School, Arkansas.

elastic clause Reference to the **necessary and proper clause** of
the US **constitution**. It is deemed 'elastic' due to the legislative flexibility these words have given **Congress**.

electoral college The body that, ultimately, decides who
becomes **President** of the United States. Rather than this
post being directly elected by the people, it is a majority
of votes within the electoral college that presidential candidates have to win. Each state is allocated a number of
delegates to this body equal to their representation in
Congress. More populous states therefore have greater
representation than smaller states. Delegates of the
college vote every four years in their respective state

capitols, and the results of this ballot are communicated to the Congress, where the **Vice President** (as president of the Senate) will announce the result. The candidate who wins a majority of the electoral college votes becomes President.

The democratic link between the college's decision and the result of the popular vote in the November **general election** is reflected in whom the delegates vote for. In modern times, all the delegates from a state will vote for the candidate who received the largest popular vote in their state. Only Maine differs from this 'winner takes all' formula. Here, the delegates vote proportionally. It has been rare for delegates to abandon this practice and cast a vote that does not mirror the popular vote in their own state.

However, due to the indirect manner in which the presidential race is decided, occasionally the candidate who wins the greatest number of popular votes nation-wide fails to gain a majority of the delegates' votes in the electoral college. This was the fate of Andrew Jackson (1824), Samuel Tilden (1876), Grover Cleveland (1888), and Al Gore (2000). In these instances, although the can-didates had successfully won over the majority of the people, these votes were not spread sufficiently amongst all of the states. Supporters of the electoral college system cite this as being important in a federal system: the President should be the choice of a wide range of states, and not just the majority of the people. The college's opponents consider the system anachronistic, and a number of unsuccessful attempts have been made to amend the **constitution**, replacing the electoral college with a direct popular election.

Emancipation Proclamation President Abraham **Lincoln's** **civil war** declaration to the south that the US government would free all slaves resident in states still in rebellion on 1 January 1863. Although the federal government had to win the civil war to enforce this emancipation, the proclamation gave notice that the civil war was to be fought over the issue of slavery as well as the right of **secession**. The end of slavery in the United States was confirmed by the **ratification** of the **Thirteenth Amendment** to the **constitution** in 1865.

emergency powers see **state of emergency**

EMILY's List An interest group campaigning to help **pro-choice** Democratic women win political office at both the state and federal level. Women matching these criteria are helped by EMILY with funding and technical support. EMILY is an acronym for the organisation's strategy: 'Early Money Is Like Yeast' (that is, it helps the dough rise). Women candidates who receive financial backing in the early stages of their campaign are more successful in attracting additional backers, and therefore more likely to get elected.

Website: http://www.emilyslist.org

enumerated powers see **delegated powers**

equal rights amendment An amendment to the US **constitution**, first proposed in 1923, which would outlaw discrimination on the grounds of sex. This potential amendment, despite being on the political agenda for so long, and having been approved by the US **Congress**, has yet to be ratified by the requisite number of states. Opponents to the change argue that the constitution already protects women as equals, while its supporters state that, as sexual discrimination still remains a feature of US society, the amendment is specifically required, just as the Fourteenth Amendment outlaws racial discrimination.

Website: http://www.equalrightsamendment.org

establishment clause The **First Amendment** to the US **constitution** states that 'Congress shall make no law respecting the establishment of religion'. This establishment clause has traditionally prevented governments in the United States from promoting religious activities. The **Supreme Court**, for example, has prohibited the holding of morning prayers in public schools. With the rise of the **Christian Right,** however, arguments for governments being able to support religious activities has been growing. Opponents of the traditional interpretation of the establishment clause contend that as long as one religion is not officially endorsed over another, then interaction between governments and religion should be permitted.

executive agencies The federal departments and **independent agencies** established by the **President** of the United States to carry out the functions of the **executive branch** of government.

executive branch A division of government charged with implementing acts passed by the **legislative branch**. In modern times, executives around the world have also taken more responsibility for proposing policy. The **President** heads the executive branch of the US **federal government**. This individual is responsible for executing federal law, managing the foreign affairs of the United States, and commanding the country's armed forces. In order to carry out these duties, the President is served by a bureaucracy consisting of **cabinet** departments, **independent agencies**, and military institutions. In total, the executive branch employs over two million civilian workers and 1.5 million military personnel.

Website: http://www.firstgov.gov/Agencies/Federal/Executive.shtml

Executive Office of the President The division of the federal **executive branch**, created in 1939 by Franklin D. Roosevelt, which hosts the **President's White House** staff and senior policy advisors. Included within the Executive Office, for example, are the **National Security Council** and the National Economic Council.

Website: http://www.firstgov.gov/Agencies/Federal/Executive.shtml

executive order Edicts issued by the **President** of the United States that have the force of law provided they are founded on the President's constitutional powers, or are already powers granted to the **chief executive** through an act of **Congress**. The President may, for example, deploy US troops for peace-keeping purposes via an executive order, or impose economic sanctions against a foreign nation. These cases are permissible because the chief executive is operating within his or her respective constitutional roles as **Commander in Chief** or **Chief Diplomat**. Executive orders may be countermanded by subsequent acts of Congress, or invalidated by the **Supreme Court** as unconstitutional (see, for example, *Youngstown Sheet and Tube Company* v. *Sawyer*, 1952).

executive privilege The right of the **President** to withhold information from the **Congress**, the federal courts, the states, or the general public. Although there is no reference to this right in the **constitution**, executive privilege is assumed on the grounds that if there were no secrecy about the deliberations of the **executive branch**, advice given to the President would not necessarily be candid or truthful. In the nineteenth century, presidents had sought to keep from Congress the details of diplomatic negotiations. In more recent years, however, the executive has more often refused to supply information because this would be 'incompatible with the national interest'. Franklin D. **Roosevelt** refused to furnish Congress with **Federal Bureau of Investigation** files, for example, while J. F. **Kennedy** ordered military officers not to testify to a Congressional committee about the **Bay of Pigs** incident. Most famously, on the grounds of executive privilege, Richard **Nixon** refused to supply the tapes of conversations recorded in the **Oval Office** to the Congressional committee investigating the **Watergate** affair. In the case of *United States* v. *Nixon,* **1974** the **Supreme Court** ruled that executive privilege did not extend to criminal investigations, and Nixon was forced to relinquish these tapes. His resignation soon followed.

F

Farewell address see **Washington's farewell address**

FBI see **Federal Bureau of Investigation**

FCC see **Federal Communications Commission**

FDR see **Franklin D. Roosevelt**

FEC see **Federal Election Commission**

FECA see **Federal Election Campaign Act, 1971**

Federal Bureau of Investigation An agency of the Department of Justice, the FBI is the main criminal investigatory arm of the **federal government**. It enforces federal laws, and cooperates with the states to provide nationwide criminal intelligence. The FBI's workload is as varied as federal legislation itself, ranging from aircraft piracy to the protection of civil rights. Any crime that crosses state borders also comes under the jurisdiction of the Bureau, while the FBI has also traditionally been involved in counter-insurgency and counter-terrorism on American soil. The organisation has its headquarters in Washington DC, which is complemented by a number of field offices throughout the USA. In certain specialist areas of investigation, the FBI defers to other agencies of the Department of Justice, such as the Drug Enforcement Administration, the Immigration and Naturalisation Service, and the Bureau of Alcohol, Tobacco, Firearms and Explosives.

Website: http://www.fbi.gov

Federal Communications Commission The FCC, established in 1934, is the federal regulatory body that supervises broadcasting in the United States.

Website: http://www.fcc.gov

Federal Election Campaign Act, 1971 (FECA) Legislation that attempted to bring a degree of transparency to campaign finance, and address the issue of money in US politics. Candidates in federal elections were now required to disclose the source of most of their contributions. An amendment to the act in 1974 established the Federal Election Commission to oversee this disclosure process. This amendment also sought to place a ceiling on how much a candidate could spend on a campaign, and limited the sum of money an individual or organisation could give to any one candidate. Individual contributions were restricted to US$1,000, while organisations could donate no more than US$5,000. FECA additionally offered public funds to federal candidates.

This initial attempt at campaign finance reform, although successful in many respects, did not solve the problem of money in US federal elections. Although the disclosure element of the act stood, the **Supreme Court** ruled that candidates should not be restricted in the amount of money they spend on their own campaign (unless they accepted public money). The case of *Buckley* v. *Valeo,* 1976 stated this would be a violation of a candidate's political expression, and thus an infringement of the **First Amendment**. Similarly, while the Court supported a limit being placed on donations directly to campaigns (**hard money**), no such ceiling should be placed on US citizens spending money on political activities *independent* of these official campaigns (**soft money**). There should be no restrictions on the buying of airtime, for example, to express a view that did not directly advocate the election of a particular candidate.

This ruling ushered in a new era of electioneering, dominated by the use of soft money on **issue advertisements**. It was not until 2002, and the **Bipartisan Campaign Reform Act**, that Congress again attempted to reform campaign finance, and to close some of these loopholes.

Federal Election Commission Created by a 1974 amendment to the **Federal Election Campaign Act, 1971**, the FEC is an independent regulatory agency that oversees laws governing federal elections in the United States. It is involved in advising upon, and auditing, the disclosure of campaign contributions, as well as managing the public funding of presidential candidates.

Website: http://www.fec.gov

federal government The term used to refer to the central, national government of the United States, based primarily in **Washington DC**. The federal government differs from the fifty state governments in that it has a national **jurisdiction**, and it governs in separate policy areas from those of the states

federal pre-emption Where a federal law or policy gains precedence over state legislation.

Federal Reserve System A body established by **Congress** in 1913, which acts as the US national bank. It is this agency that sets the interest rate for the twelve Federal Reserve Banks.
Website: http://www.federalreserve.gov

federalism A system of government where power and responsibilities are divided between a national authority and several regional units. The United States is a political formation of fifty individual state governments and one federal administration with a national **jurisdiction**. The US **constitution** dictates which powers are delegated to the central government (see **delegated powers**), which are reserved by the states (see **reserved powers**), and which are denied to any government, and remain the sovereign rights of individual citizens (see **denied powers**). Despite this constitutional guidance, the relationship between the **federal government** and the states has not remained constant over time. The traditional balance of **dual federalism,** where the state and federal authorities largely governed in distinct and separate areas, gave way to **cooperative federalism** with Franklin D. **Roosevelt's New Deal** in the 1930s. From this point in history, the federal government has initiated and funded programmes in areas traditionally under the jurisdiction of the states.

President Lyndon B. **Johnson** even talked of a **creative federalism** in the 1960s, which involved even greater levels of federal intervention. Since the 1970s, however, there have been attempts to return power back to the states. This has been termed **new federalism**.

Federalist Papers A series of eighty-five articles published in *The Federalist* newspaper between 1787 and 1788. Written under the pseudonym 'Publius', these essays were the works of Alexander **Hamilton**, James **Madison**, and John Jay, aimed at persuading the individual states of the union to ratify the newly negotiated **constitution**. Although these articles were only part of a much wider exchange of tracts and letters in the American press at this time, both supporting and opposing **ratification**, collectively these essays, over time, have come to represent an almost sacred defence and explanation of the values of the US constitution. Even today, lawyers and politicians pore over these works to find justifications and advice on contemporary political disputes and policy decisions. Federalist papers numbers 10 and 51, written by Madison, for example, form one of the most logical and convincing defences of pluralism, while Hamilton's paper number 78 argues for the need of judicial review within any liberal government.

Federalists A term used to describe various political factions formed early in US history. Originally the title was given to supporters of the **constitution** penned in Philadelphia. Both Alexander **Hamilton** and Thomas **Jefferson**, for example, campaigned for this document to be ratified by the states. Their opponents were termed anti-federalists. Confusingly, however, the title 'federalist' came to mean something different a few years later. Even as early as

George **Washington**'s first term of office, Hamilton was described as a federalist because he favoured a strong central government. Jefferson, on the other hand, was no longer a federalist because he advocated a diffusion of power.

Fifth Amendment The **constitutional amendment** that guarantees citizens **due process of law** should they be accused of a crime. In particular, this passage of the US **constitution** prevents individuals from being tried for the same crime more than once (**double jeopardy**), and gives them a right to silence. The Fifth Amendment also states that no citizen may have their property taken without due compensation. This is one of the ten amendments that collectively form the **Bill of Rights**.

filibuster A method of obstructing the legislative process by extending its debating stage indefinitely. Prior to 1917, US senators had the right of unlimited debate when considering a bill. This made it possible for opponents of a piece of legislation to effectively talk the measure off the **floor** of the **Senate**. They would filibuster, refusing to stop debating, thus preventing the issue reaching a vote. In the meantime, the Senate was prevented from moving on to any other business. A bill's sponsors would thus be forced to withdraw their bill in order that the Senate could once more function normally. Filibustering is an effective way for a minority to block the wishes of the majority. In 1917, the Senate's rules were amended to allow a motion of **cloture** to be passed, where, if there is agreement of three-fifths of members, debate is ended, and a bill proceeds immediately to a vote. This change of rules has made filibustering harder to organise, but the practice still continues as it is often difficult to persuade sixty of the one hundred-member Senate (three-fifths) to support a motion of cloture. The **House of Representatives** has no problems with filibustering, as its debates are all time constrained.

fireside chats A series of radio broadcasts presented by Franklin D. **Roosevelt**. These talks were characterised by a warm, informal tone, aimed to instil confidence and explain government policy during the harsh years of the 1930s depression. This is one of the first examples of a **President** using broadcast media to communicate directly with the people.

First Amendment The First Amendment of the US **constitution** gives citizens the right to freedom of speech, freedom of worship, and freedom of assembly. This constitutional amendment also guarantees the freedom of the media in the United States, and prohibits links between church and state. This is one of the ten amendments that collectively form the **Bill of Rights**.

First Lady The wife of the **President** of the United States. Although this person holds no formal office or salary, Presidents' partners have become more politically active and influential over time. Eleanor Roosevelt, for example, was a politically active journalist and visited many **New Deal** projects, reporting back to her husband (and was later appointed as a US delegate to the United Nations by Harry S. **Truman**); Lady Bird Johnson was the first presidential wife to campaign alone on behalf of her husband; Rosalynn Carter acted as a staff aide in her husband's administration; Nancy Reagan promoted an anti-drug campaign; Barbara Bush addressed the issue of illiteracy in the United States; while Hillary Clinton was involved at the highest level of policy-making with respect to welfare reforms.

527 groups A 527 is a non-profit organisation formed under Section 527 of the US Internal Revenue Code, which grants tax-exempt status to political committees at the national, state and local level. Although these groups have been around for some time, they gained more significance after the passage of the **Bipartisan Campaign Reform Act, 2002.** Given that this legislation limited the opportunities for **soft money** donations to political parties and campaigns, these 527 groups now play a greater part in campaign finance strategies. By definition, the 527s are legally independent of parties and official campaigns, and therefore targets for soft money. Unlike **political action committees**, they are permitted to raise unrestricted sums of soft money for political activity, as long as this money is not used to specifically endorse victory or defeat of an election candidate. In 2004, for example, the 527 group Swift Boat Veterans for Truth ran **issue advertisements** on national television questioning **Democratic Party** presidential nominee John Kerry's **Vietnam War** record. Although these 'issue ads' made no mention of Kerry's opponent George W. **Bush,** this publicity helped the latter's presidential campaign considerably. 527s are now a major conduit of soft money.

flexible construction An elastic interpretation of a legal document. A judge or politician that subjects the US **constitution** to flexible construction will seek to make this nineteenth century tract relevant to modern life. Rather than adhering to literal definitions of the words, they will seek timeless principles in the language, and apply these to today's society. The opposite of flexible construction is **strict construction**.

See also: **living constitution**

floor Reference to when a legislative body meets as a whole, to debate a bill. For example: 'The committee reported the proposal to the floor of the **Senate**'.

floor manager Once a bill has been reported by a Congressional committee to the **floor** of either the **Senate** or **House of Representatives**, a member of that chamber will be assigned to guide it through the legislative process. This individual will attempt to make sure the bill gains support amongst colleagues and no crippling amendments are placed upon it.

food stamps Government tokens provided to those on low income, and without savings, which can be exchanged for groceries in shops across the United States. Food stamp initiatives started in the **Great Depression** years of the 1930s, but no permanent programme existed until 1964. The 1970s saw a dramatic rise in the number of stamps issued. The programme is currently co-ordinated at the federal level by the US Department of Agriculture (specifically through its agency: the Food and Nutrition Service), while state bodies administer the programme at the local level. In 2004, over 23 million persons were in receipt of food stamps.

Ford, Gerald R. (1913–) **President** of the United States between 1974 and 1977. Gerald Rudolph Ford turned down the opportunity to play American football professionally in order to study at Yale Law School and serve in the US Navy during the Second World War. Discharged as a Lieutenant-Commander at the end of this conflict, Ford returned to his home town of Grand Rapids, Michigan, to practise law. After a short period of activity in local **Republican Party** politics, he was elected to the US **House of Representatives** in 1948.

Continually re-elected by his constituency, Ford became House **minority leader** in 1965. It was from this position that Ford took an unusual path to the US presidency.

With the resignation of Spiro **Agnew** in 1973, Richard **Nixon** nominated Ford to be his new **Vice President**. This appointment was confirmed by both chambers of Congress, in accordance with the provisions of the **Twenty-fifth Amendment**. Ford was then elevated to the presidency itself in 1974, when Nixon also resigned, over the **Watergate** affair. This makes Ford the only individual to serve as **President** of the United States without having been elected either as President or Vice President.

Controversially, one of Ford's first acts as President was to pardon Richard Nixon for any crimes he may have committed related to the Watergate incident, an act that outraged many Americans. Ford similarly had difficulty winning over a Democratic majority **Congress**, which after **mid-term elections** had the ability to override Ford's many presidential **vetoes**. In terms of domestic policy, the Ford Administration attempted to cope with inflation and economic recession. In the foreign arena, Ford's watch coincided with the fall of Cambodia to the Khmer Rouge, and the evacuation of remaining US troops from Vietnam. Despite Watergate, economic stagflation, and these foreign policy setbacks, it is notable that Ford only narrowly lost to Jimmy **Carter** in the 1976 presidential election.

forty acres and a mule Faced with the massive dislocation of African-Americans during the latter stages of the **civil war**, General William Sherman of the Union army issued Special Field Order Number Fifteen, which promised freed slaves 'forty acres and a mule' (i.e. land and a means of farming this land). Presumably this land was to be confiscated from white farmers who supported the **Confederation of American States**. In fact, this order only applied to black families within Sherman's vicinity, on the coast of Georgia and Florida, and was a temporary measure. However, the idea of 'forty acres and a mule' resonated widely amongst ex-slaves, and raised their hopes that economic equality would result in the south as a result of **reconstruction**. In reality, few, if any, African-Americans received such support from the **federal government**. 'Forty acres and a mule' has thus became a rallying cry for **civil rights** campaigners across the years, highlighting the fact that African-Americans are still waiting for equality.

Frankfurter, Felix (1882–1965) Appointed by **President** Franklin D. **Roosevelt,** Frankfurter served as a **Supreme Court** justice between 1939 and 1962. He was a leading advocate of **judicial restraint**.

free exercise clause Reference to the First Amendment of the US **constitution**, which states that 'Congress shall make no law respecting the establishment of religion, or prohibiting the free exercise thereof'. This free exercise clause underwrites Americans' rights to express religious belief uninhibited by the state.

fruit-cake federalism Cake analogies have been used to describe the differing forms of **federalism** found in the United States over time: **layer-cake federalism** for **dual federalism;** and **marble-cake federalism** for **cooperative federalism**. 'Fruit-cake federalism' refers to a system where the overlaps and duplications between federal and state governments have become dense and unmanageable, yet provide 'sweets' for everyone.

G

GAO see **General Accounting Office**

Garcia v. *San Antonio Metropolitan Transit Authority*, 1985
A **Supreme Court** judgment that confirmed the right of **Congress** to include state and local government employees within the remit of national minimum wage and labour rights legislation. The San Antonio Transit Authority had argued that the **federal government** had no **jurisdiction** in this area of local government. The Court, however, disagreed. It ruled that the **commerce clause** applied in this case. In many respects, *Garcia* represents the high-water mark of the Supreme Court favouring the commerce clause, and federal intervention, over state sovereignty. The Court's later ruling of *United States* v. *Lopez*, 1995, for example, although it did not purport to overturn *Garcia*, signalled the Court's intention to set limits with respect to Congress' authority in areas traditionally regarded as within the jurisdiction of the states.

General Accountability Office see **General Accounting Office**

General Accounting Office An agency of the US **Congress**, established in 1921 to help this body oversee the work of the **executive branch**. The GAO conducts, on behalf of Congress, audits of federal budgets, investigations of legislation implementation, and analyses policies emerging from the executive. In 2004, the GAO was renamed the General Accountability Office.
Website: http://www.gao.gov

general election Defined, in the United States, as a series of elections, involving candidates from competing parties, held nationwide. General elections are organised on the first Tuesday in November, every twenty-four months, in even-numbered years. These elections are distinct from **primary elections**, in that they involve candidates from different parties competing for political office. They are not intra-party contests (i.e. primaries). Similarly, general elections involve numerous concurrent polls across the whole USA, and are not just confined to one or a few constituencies.

general revenue sharing A policy in place between 1972 and 1986 where a proportion of revenue raised by the **federal government** was given directly to state and local governments.

Gettysburg Address The speech given by **President** Abraham **Lincoln** in 1863, commemorating those who had died in the Battle of Gettysburg earlier in the **civil war**. He argued that, for these individuals not to have lost their lives in vain, the United States needed to rebuild itself on the principles of freedom and democracy. This short speech is regarded by many as one of the greatest expressions of democratic ideals, and contains the famous phrase that government should be 'of the people, by the people, for the people'.

***Gideon* v. *Wainwright*, 1963** A **Supreme Court** decision that requires all courts in the United States to appoint free legal representation to those facing the possibility of a prison sentence. This applies if the accused cannot afford to hire their own trial lawyer. Clarence Gideon was sentenced to five years incarceration by the state of Florida for the crime of burglary. He was forced to defend himself at his trial, as Florida courts, at the time, only provided court-appointed legal counsel to those accused of capital crimes (that is, crimes that carry the possibility of a death sentence). Gideon successfully argued before the Supreme Court that this denial of legal representation, given that he could not afford his own lawyer, violated his rights of **due process** guaranteed by the Sixth and Fourteenth Amendments to the US **constitution**. At his re-trial, now assisted by a court-appointed lawyer, Gideon was found not guilty of the original burglary charge.

Gingrich, Newt (1943–) Newton Leroy Gingrich is a conservative **Republican Party** politician from the state of Georgia. He served as **Speaker of the House of Representatives** between 1995 and 1999, and used this position to orchestrate the Republican revolution based on the **Contract with America**. This 'revolution' attempted to push through an alternative conservative policy agenda, usurping **President** Bill **Clinton's** own legislative programme. A combative relationship between the **Congress** and the **executive branch** culminated in Gingrich calling for Clinton's **impeachment** over the Monica **Lewinsky** affair and the financial irregularities of **Whitewater**. By late 1998, however, Gingrich's confrontational style, and revelations of an extra-martial affair of his own, were seen as electoral liabilities by many fellow Republicans. Gingrich subsequently resigned not only as Speaker, but from the House of Representatives altogether. Still active in conservative politics, Gingrich is tipped as a potential future presidential candidate.

GOP see **Grand Old Party**

governor The title given to the head of the **executive branch** (that is, the **chief executive**) of individual state governments. Governors are directly elected, and enjoy state powers similar to those of the President of the United States within the federal government: the right to veto legislation; commander in chief of the state national guard; and the ability to grant legal pardons, for example.

Gramm-Rudman-Hollings see **national debt**

Grand Old Party The 'Grand Old Party' or 'GOP' is an alias for the **Republican Party** used since the 1870s.

grants-in-aid Most commonly, a reference to the sums of money the **federal government** transfers to state and local governments in order to fund specific policies, in the areas of health, education and welfare provision, for example.

Great Compromise see **connecticut Compromise**

Great Depression A period of economic downturn that started with the New York stock market crash of 1929, and lasted until World War Two stimulated global markets once more. Many investors lost their savings during the depression, numerous banks closed, production slumped, and unemployment grew to record figures. The political response to this hardship was the election of **President** Franklin D. **Roosevelt** in 1932, who aimed to mitigate the consequences of the depression with his **New Deal**.

Great Society reforms A programme of legislation initiated by **President** Lyndon B. **Johnson**, during the 1960s, aimed at tackling poverty and racial discrimination in the United States. Johnson, seeking a 'great society', allocated federal money to provide educational opportunities, improve the health, and address the general welfare

of poor communities in the USA. The federal programmes of **Medicare** and **Medicaid**, for example, date
back to this era. In terms of tackling racial discrimination, the Johnson Administration secured the passage of
the **Civil Rights Act** of 1964, which attacked racial segregation in public spaces, schools and the workplace,
together with the **Voting Rights Act** of 1965, which outlawed the literacy tests used to prevent African-
Americans from voting in the southern states. Although
the **Vietnam War** diverted resources and attention away
from the Great Society programme, this series of reforms
still forms the foundation of much of the US welfare
system today.

gubernatorial A word meaning 'of, or pertaining to, a governor'. A gubernatorial election, for example, will decide
which candidate will become governor of a state.

Gulf of Tonkin The location of two allegedly unprovoked
attacks by North Vietnamese torpedo boats on US Navy
ships during 1964. In response to this incident, **Congress**
passed the Gulf of Tonkin Resolution, granting **President**
Lyndon B. **Johnson** support to protect US forces in this
region. This resolution would later be interpreted by the
Johnson Administration as constitutional authorisation
to escalate US military operations in Vietnam.

gun control see **Second Amendment**

H

Hamilton, Alexander (*c.*1755–1804) Having served with dis-
tinction in George **Washington**'s army during the **War of
Independence**, Hamilton became an influential politician

during the early period of United States history. He was a member of the **Continental Congress,** and a key advocate of abandoning the **Articles of Confederation** in favour of a stronger **federal government.** In this respect, Hamilton was appointed as a delegate representing the state of New York at the Philadelphia constitutional congress. Alongside James **Madison** and John Jay, Hamilton then co-authored the **Federalist Papers** in support of the new constitution, successfully convincing the states to ratify this document. In government, Hamilton served as the first Secretary of the Treasury between 1789 and 1795, and then, on the formation of political parties, became a powerful member of the **Federalist Party.** He continued to advocate a strong role for the national government. Hamilton was to die after a duel in 1804, being shot by a political rival Aaron Burr, after allegedly questioning this individual's honour at a dinner party.

hanging chad A faulty, partially pierced hole made in a ballot paper punch card. **Chad**s came to the attention of the world during the 2000 **general election,** when George W. **Bush** narrowly beat Al Gore to become **President** of the United States. Legal action challenging Bush's victory focused on the inadequacy of the state of Florida's automated electoral equipment, which had produced significant numbers of faulty hanging chads on ballot cards, instead of chads. The outcome of this legal action effectively decided who would be President. The US **Supreme Court's** decision *Bush* v. *Gore,* 2000 denied Gore the right to a manual recount of the Florida ballot cards. The original machine-read result, and Bush's victory, stood.

hard money A phrase used to describe financial contributions to political campaigns that are used *directly* to elect candidates. Such expenditure is tightly regulated by campaign finance law, with the amount of hard money a campaign may receive from any one individual or organisation being capped. By contrast, **soft money** contributions are not so tightly controlled, but these may only be used to fund political activity not advocating the election of a candidate.

Hearings, Congressional see **Congressional hearings**

Heart of Atlanta Motel v. *United States*, 1964 A **Supreme Court** ruling confirming the **Civil Rights Act, 1964** to be constitutional. Supporters of **segregation** in the southern states, having failed to block the Civil Rights Act in the US **Congress**, mounted a legal challenge against its provisions. The **appellant** contested that the **federal government** had no right to impose desegregation on his business. It was argued that since this motel was privately owned, and operated solely within the state of Georgia, it had the right to refuse guests on the grounds of colour if it so wished. The federal government had no **jurisdiction** in this area. The Supreme Court disagreed. It was of the **opinion** that the motel was open to out-of-state guests, due to its location near interstate highways, and thus came under the federal jurisdiction of **interstate commerce**. The Civil Rights Act was deemed constitutional.

Homeland Security, Department of see **Department of Homeland Security**

Hoover, J. Edgar (1895–1972) Hoover served as the Director of the **Federal Bureau of Investigation** between 1924 and 1972. Almost fifty years at the helm of the FBI saw Hoover build this agency into a professional body of law enforcement. Hoover's strategies of crime fighting, however, were not without controversy. He collected damaging information on politicians, and kept this intelligence under his own personal control. These secret files were used to maintain himself in post as the FBI's director, and he was apparently able to intimidate even sitting presidents by threatening to leak damaging disclosures. By the early 1970s Hoover had come under public criticism for his authoritarian administration of the FBI and for his persecution of those he personally regarded as radicals and subversives. Similarly questions were being asked about the FBI's failure to tackle Mafia crime. Despite these criticisms, Hoover remained in office until his death in 1972.

Hopper The wooden box located on the **floor** of the **House of Representatives** in which members place draft legislation they wish to introduce to this chamber. The **Senate** has no equivalent receptacle. Instead, draft bills are simply handed to a clerk.

House of Representatives The lower chamber of the US **Congress**. Members stand for election every 2 years, and represent 435 nationwide constituencies of approximately equal population. In addition, four non-voting **delegates to the House of Representatives** sit in the chamber, attending to the interests of the territories of American Samoa, the **District of Columbia**, Guam, and the Virgin Islands, along with the Resident Commissioner of Puerto Rico.

The House is traditionally seen as the 'popular' chamber of the Congress, members having always been directly and regularly elected by the general public. Consequently, Representatives tend to focus closely on their constituency's interests, making sure, perhaps more than the **Senate**, that their district has a voice in national (and international) affairs. Given this closeness to the people, the US **constitution** vests certain exclusive powers to the House of Representatives, among the most important of which are the right to initiate impeachment proceedings and the right to originate revenue bills.

The work and organisation of the House is dominated by the **committee system**.

Website: http://www.house.gov

House of Representatives Committee on Appropriations
Article One, Section Nine of the US **constitution** states that 'No money shall be drawn from the treasury, but in consequence of appropriations made by law . . .' Originally undertaken by the **House of Representatives Committee on Ways and Means,** since 1865, this allocation of money has been the task of the House Appropriations Committee. Any spending of federal funds has to be first approved by this body. The committee therefore scrutinises all legislation proposed by other committees, making sure government money is being spent appropriately. This control of the purse strings makes this particular committee very powerful.

Website: http://appropriations.house.gov

House of Representatives Committee on Rules see **rules committees**

House of Representatives Committee on Ways and Means
Given that the US **constitution** vests exclusive power with respect to revenue bills with the House of Representatives, this makes the Ways and Means Committee one of the most powerful bodies in the US **Congress**. This body enjoys a broad jurisdiction over bills linked to taxation. The committee therefore makes important policy decisions with respect to federal

welfare, education, health and economic programmes, for example.

Website: http://waysandmeans.house.gov

hyphenated-Americans Reference to the fact that many in the United States pay attention to the ethnic origin of individuals, even several generations after their families originally arrived in this country. Thus individuals and communities become sub-categories of Americans, proceeded by a hyphen: African-Americans, Italian-Americans, Irish-Americans, and so on.

I

impeachment The act of charging a public official with misconduct, and determining whether or not they should be removed from office. In the case of **federal government** employees, it is the US **Congress** that prosecutes the impeachment process. Proceedings are initiated in the Judiciary Committee of the **House of Representatives**. This body holds **hearings** on the allegations, and then reports to the **floor** of the House on whether an individual should answer to charges of 'treason, bribery or other high crimes and misdemeanours' (Article Three of the US **constitution**). The House, after debating this report, collectively determines whether impeachment is appropriate with a simple majority vote. If it is deemed that charges are warranted, Articles of Impeachment are drawn up, and passed over to the US **Senate**.

Senators collectively act as a court to judge the charges brought by the House. The **Chief Justice** of the **Supreme Court** presides. A guilty verdict requires a two-thirds majority vote. Conviction will result in this official being removed from post, and the Senate may also bar them from future public office. Congress has no power to invoke criminal penalties on those found guilty, although additional legal charges may follow from law enforcement agencies.

Congress traditionally reserves the impeachment process for significant cases of alleged misconduct. Of the sixty-two individuals investigated by the House since 1797, sixteen have been impeached by this chamber, and seven of those convicted and removed from office by the Senate (all the guilty parties being judges). The House has voted to impeach two **Presidents** during this period: Andrew Johnson (1868) and Bill **Clinton** (1999). Johnson survived conviction in the Senate by one vote, while the charges against Clinton were dismissed by a large majority. Most famously, President Richard **Nixon** avoided being impeached by resigning from office in 1974, over the **Watergate** affair. In Nixon's case, the House of Representatives Committee on the Judiciary recommended to the floor of the House that Articles of Impeachment be drawn up, but Nixon vacated the **White House** before a floor vote could confirm impeachment. Congress may not impeach an individual after they have left office.

imperial president A term used to describe a **President** who bends or ignores constitutional **checks and balances** in order to dominate the **federal government**. Thus an imperial president relies on **White House** aides rather than consulting **cabinet** colleagues or members of **Congress**. They also actively resist **oversight** from other branches of government. Decision-making becomes more secretive and centred on the president's own 'court', or 'inner circle', rather than being a transparent, open process, involving consultation. Various **chief executives** have been accused of being 'imperial presidents'. Lyndon

B. **Johnson,** for example, for the way in which he committed US forces to Vietnam without full disclosure to Congress, or Ronald **Reagan** and his secret war in Latin America that led to the **Irangate** scandal. The presidency of Richard **Nixon,** however, is most closely associated with this term, given his lack of respect for Congress and political opponents, which bordered on criminal activity, as evidenced by the **Watergate** affair.

Further reading: Arthur Schlesinger, *The Imperial Presidency* (Boston, MA: Houghton Mifflin, 1973)

implied powers Those powers that, although not specifically referred to in the US **constitution,** are deemed to be a logical extension or an implication of this document. The US **Congress,** for example, passed legislation that established a national bank in 1791. Nowhere in the **constitution** is there a clause that specifically permits the **federal government** to charter banks. Congress' authority in this area is thus an 'implied power'. As the constitution charges Congress with regulating the borrowing of money, and the minting of currency on behalf of the United States, the formation of a national bank was therefore accepted as a logical extension of this role (see *McCulloch* v. *Maryland,* **1819**). Many of the implied powers are constitutionally justified by the **necessary and proper clause** and the **commerce clause.**

inauguration Ceremonies that mark the start of a new political term. The US **president's** inauguration traditionally consists of a formal oath of office given before the **Chief Justice,** followed by a speech to the nation outlining the administration's plans for the coming four years (the 'inaugural address'). Numerous 'inaugural balls' or parties are then held across **Washington DC,** in the evening, celebrating the new (or renewed) political order.

incumbent The individual currently holding a political post is the 'incumbent'. Where an incumbent is repeatedly re-appointed or re-elected to office this may create a problem for good government. Challengers are dissuaded from competing for power, while new policy ideas that new personnel would bring to an office may now fail to reach decision-making forums. This problem of incumbency is often compounded by the fact that incumbents, through simply occupying an office, often gain an advantage over their opponents. They are able to gain greater publicity for their campaigns, as well as being able to raise more **campaign finance**.

independent agencies Predominately, units of the **executive branch** that operate independently of the main federal departments. These smaller executive agencies are charged with implementing specific elements of public policy. The **Central Intelligence Agency**, for example, is an independent agency, operating apart from the Departments of State and Defense, reporting directly to the **President** via the **National Security Council**. Other independent agencies include the **Federal Communications Commission**, the National Aeronautics and Space Commission (NASA), and the United States Postal Service. **Congress** also supervises a number of independent agencies of its own, which help it with the legislative process: the **Government Accountability Office**, for example, and the Library of Congress.

Website: http://www.firstgov.gov/Agencies/Federal/Independent.shtml

indirect primary A **primary election** where the victorious delegate is under no obligation to vote for a particular candidate at the **national party convention**. With a direct primary, by contrast, winners are bound to vote for the candidate he or she pledged to support whilst campaigning to be a delegate.

inherent powers see **implied powers**

initiative election A referendum on an issue initiated by a group of citizens. Once a specified number of citizens register their support for an initiative, this policy is put before the electorate as a whole for a decision. Many local and state governments in the US make provision for citizens to introduce legislation via such initiative elections.

Inland Revenue Service The IRS is a bureau of the **Department of the Treasury** responsible for collecting federal taxes in the United States, and enforcing tax law.
    Website: http://www.irs.gov

intentionalist see **strict construction**

interstate commerce clause see **commerce clause**

Iran-Contra scandal see **Irangate**

Irangate A scandal that disrupted the Reagan Administration in 1986. A Congressional and media investigation revealed that **National Security Council** (NSC) officials had secretly sold arms to Iran. The sale was arranged on the basis that it would strengthen the position of moderates within the Iranian regime who, in turn, could help secure the release of western hostages. The money generated by the arms sale was then used by the NSC to fund the right-wing Contra rebel movement in Nicaragua. Not only was this arms sale questionable on the grounds of the United States providing weapons to Iran, a country that posed a direct security threat to the US, it also contravened specific Congressional legislation that banned the **executive branch** from providing military aid to the Contra rebel movement. Questions were asked over the extent to which **President** Ronald **Reagan**, and other high-ranking executive officials, knew about this operation. The outcome of this investigation, however, was that just two members of the NSC, Admiral John Poindexter and Colonel Oliver **North**, were tried and convicted in the courts.

iron triangle A phrase used to signify the mutual supporting relationships that can develop between legislators, bureaucrats and interest groups. It is charged that an iron triangle formed by these three parties prioritises securing each party's interests, rather than serving the public good. It is an 'iron' triangle because it is difficult for 'outsiders' to penetrate these established policy networks.

IRS see **Inland Revenue Service**

isolationism A policy of standing aloof from international affairs. Most prominently, the United States took an isolationist stance during the 1920s and 1930s, officially remaining neutral in the run-up to World War Two. This isolationist era was ended by **President** Franklin D. **Roosevelt**, who declared war on Germany and Japan after the attack on Pearl Harbor in 1941.

issue advertisements Issue ads are advertisements that seek to highlight a particular position or policy, but do not overtly call for the election of a particular candidate. They have been used extensively in recent years by political parties and interest groups in their efforts to circumvent **campaign finance** laws.

J

Jackson, Andrew (1767–1845) Seventh **President** of the United States, holding office between 1829 and 1837. Born in the frontier territory of the Carolinas, Jackson served, aged fourteen, in George **Washington**'s continental army, against the British, in the **War of Independence**. After the war, he built a successful career as a lawyer in Tennessee. It was his later military exploits, however, that caught the public's imagination. Leading US troops between 1812 and 1818, he first defeated Creek Indian forces allied to Britain in Alabama, and then British and Spanish forces in the south-east of the country. These military exploits hastened the incorporation of Florida, formerly a Spanish possession, into the United States. After an unsuccessful bid to become President of the United States in 1824, due to the vagaries of the **electoral college**, he was eventually elected to the White House in 1828.

Jackson spent most of his presidency rearranging the **federal government** and contending with **Congress**. His accomplishments were mostly negative: relocating Indian tribes west of the Mississippi, vetoing road bills and a Bank bill, and opposing nullification (a movement where states asserted their right to **veto** federal legislation). The greatest achievement of his administration, the rise of the mass political party (the **Democratic Party**), was more the work of advisors than of Jackson himself.

He did, however, make a lasting imprint on US history, as a war hero, and the first president 'of the people', who represented the nation as a whole, and not isolated interests.

Jefferson, Thomas (1743–1826) Third **President** of the United States, holding office between 1801 and 1809. The son of a wealthy Virginian tobacco-plantation owner, Thomas

Jefferson played a major role in the founding, and the politics of the early years, of the United States. He was the main author of the **Declaration of Independence**; he was a member of the **Continental Congress**; he led the Democratic-Republican Party; was elected **Governor** of Virginia; served as Minister to France; and was appointed **Vice President**, before becoming President himself. At the same time, Jefferson also excelled in archaeology, architecture, geography, meteorology, mathematics, music, and the sciences, amongst other fields.

The keystones of Jefferson's presidency were the imposition of strict political neutrality within the **judicial branch** of government, the abolition of interstate taxation, a reduction of the armed forces, the enhancement of states' rights over the federal government, and the **Louisiana Purchase**.

Jim Crow laws Reference to legislation passed by state governments, after the end of **reconstruction** (*c*. 1890), which sought to segregate whites and African-Americans, particularly in the south. Although, post-**civil war**, the US **constitution** outlawed direct discrimination, a series of state laws and local ordnances were enacted (Jim Crow) which prevented races mixing, on public transport, for example, or in public spaces. Similarly, African-Americans were prevented from voting. They were disfranchised by Jim Crow literacy tests (that required blacks who wished to vote to correctly recite the entire constitution, for example), and poll taxes (where a registration fee was required). These requirements were waived for white citizens. Jim Crow legislation was eventually repealed during the 1950s and 1960s, in the face of opposition from the **civil rights movement**. The phrase 'Jim Crow' derives from the song 'Jump Jim Crow', part of a popular minstrel show performed in the nineteenth century.

Johnson, Lyndon B. (1908–73) Thirty-sixth **President** of the United States, holding office between 1963 and 1969. Lyndon Baines Johnson was raised on a modest Texas ranch, and began a career in teaching during the late 1920s. Working as a volunteer in **Democratic Party** politics, he stood for office himself in 1937, and was elected to the US **House of Representatives**. Eleven years later he was returned as a US senator for the state of Texas. In a long Congressional career, Johnson built a reputation as a shrewd legislator, able to deliver votes. He served as a Democratic Party **whip**, **Senate Minority Leader**, and then the **Majority Leader**. Johnson was elected to the office of **Vice President** on John F. **Kennedy**'s presidential **ticket** in 1960, and then became President himself, in 1963, as a consequence of Kennedy's assassination. This position was confirmed in 1964, when he won a massive popular majority over his **Republican Party** opponent (Barry Goldwater) in the **general election**.

As well as providing stability to the office of the President during the politically turbulent years of the 1960s, Johnson's presidential legacy revolves around social reform, tackling racial discrimination, and the **Vietnam War**. In terms of social reform, the Johnson Administration pushed through a series of legislative provisions collectively termed the **Great Society reforms**. Alongside these laws, the **Civil Rights Act** was passed in 1964, and the **Voting Rights Act** in 1965, both of which helped end racial **segregation** in the south. These achievements, however, were overshadowed by the United States being drawn further into the Vietnam War. More American troops were committed to this conflict, despite increasing casualties and growing opposition to US involvement. In 1968, Johnson startled television viewers with a national address that included three announcements: that he had just ordered major reductions in the bombing of North Vietnam; that he was requesting peace talks; and that he would neither seek nor accept his party's nomination for re-election.

Johnson rule A rule introduced in 1953 by Lyndon B. **Johnson**, when he was **Senate Majority Leader**, that states that no **Democratic Party** senator should be awarded a second major committee assignment until all Democratic senators have received their first. This rule reformed the **seniority** system that had previously governed the **committee system** in the US **Congress**. Long-serving Democratic senators had dominated Congressional proceedings up to this point, at the expense of members more recently elected to the Senate. With this rule, committee positions would be more widely spread amongst party members.

Joint Chiefs of Staff A panel consisting of the highest-ranking officers in the US Army, Navy, Air Force and Marine Corps. The 'Joint Chiefs' act as the principal military advisors to the **President**, and other government agencies such as the Department of Defense and the **National Security Council**.
Website: http://www.jcs.mil

joint committee In the case of the US **Congress**, a committee whose membership comprises individuals from both the **Senate** and the **House of Representatives**. Joint committees are established to avoid duplication of work. These committees have been rarely used since the 1970s, with each chamber preferring to keep its independence (and foster a **separation of the powers**). Such a joint committee, however, investigated events surrounding the **Irangate** scandal of 1987.

judicial activism Where a court uses its power to interpret the law in such a way as to effectively *make* public policy. The **Supreme Court** in the 1950s and 1960s, under the leadership of Earl **Warren,** for example, interpreted the constitution in a manner that made the federal judiciary the leading policy maker on the issue of **desegregation.** The Court's decisions made **segregation** illegal in schools, public spaces and on public transport. The Warren Court was therefore 'judicially active' in this area of US politics. Those who oppose judicial activism advocate **judicial restraint.**

judicial branch The division of government charged with interpreting laws and adjudicating disputes. In the United States, each individual state has its own series of courts dealing with state laws, while federal laws are under the jurisdiction of a separate system of federal courts. All these courts recognise the ultimate authority of the US **Supreme Court,** which is the highest court of appeal, and the final interpreter of the US **constitution.**
   Website: http://www.uscourts.gov

judicial restraint Where courts hesitate from making judgments that would effectively make new public policy. A restrained court will tend to defer to legislative interpretations of the constitution, as well as those of the **executive branch.** Judicial intervention is limited to clear violations of the law. Those who think the **judicial branch** should be more dynamic in its interpretation of the constitution advocate **judicial activism.**

judicial review Where courts judge whether the acts of other branches of government are constitutional or not. Should bills passed by state legislatures or the US **Congress** be

deemed to be in conflict respectively with a state constitution or the US constitution, it is rendered null and void.
Courts may also subject the actions of state executives
and the US **President** to judicial review. Courts are the
final interpreters of constitutions, and thus have the
power to strike down legislation and policies emanating
from the other two branches of government. The power
of judicial review is not explicitly outlined in the US **constitution**, and, as such, is an **implied power**. This right
was confirmed by the **Supreme Court** decision of
Marbury v. *Madison*, 1803. This court's use of judicial
review has resulted in excess of 1,000 state laws and 120
acts of Congress being overturned since the formation of
the United States.

judicial self-restraint see **judicial restraint**

jurisdiction The area over which an institution of government
enjoys authority.

K

Kansas-Nebraska Act, 1954 see **Missouri compromise**

Kennedy, Edward (1932–) Veteran **Democratic Party**
member of **Congress**, and younger brother of **President**
John F. **Kennedy** and Robert **Kennedy**. After inheriting
his brother's Massachusetts Senate seat in 1962, 'Ted' or
'Teddy' Kennedy successfully built a power base and considerable influence within the US Congress. He has been
tipped to win the **White House** several times, but, since
1969, has never stood. Any political ambitions along
these lines would be hampered by an incident of that year
known as **Chappaquiddick**. Kennedy was charged and

found guilty of leaving the scene of an accident, after a passenger, Mary Jo Kopechne, was killed in his car, subsequent to it driving off a bridge on Chappaquiddick Island, Massachusetts.

Kennedy, John F. (1917–63) The thirty-fifth **President** of the United States, holding office between 1961 and 1963. The son of a wealthy, politically active, Massachusetts family, John Fitzgerald Kennedy was appointed US ambassador to the United Kingdom, and served in the US Navy during World War Two, before being elected to the US **House of Representatives** as a **Democratic Party** candidate in 1946. He served three terms in the House, and then became a Senator for the state of Massachusetts in 1953. Kennedy's 1960 victory against the **Republican Party** presidential candidate, Richard **Nixon**, may be noted for three particular reasons: Kennedy was the youngest person ever to be voted to the **White House**; he was the first president drawn from a Catholic background; and he secured this position by winning a greater number of votes in the **electoral college**, but not more than half of the popular vote (see **minority president**).

For many, Kennedy's youth, dynamism, charisma and good looks personify his presidency. Phrases from Kennedy's speeches are still repeated today, such as talk of the 'New Frontier', 'Ich bin ein Berliner', and 'ask not what your country can do for you, ask what you can do for your country'. Amongst this mood of renewal and reform, the Kennedy Administration laid down the foundations of far-reaching welfare and civil rights legislation that would be completed by his successor President Lyndon B. **Johnson**. Kennedy's record in foreign affairs, however, is more controversial, having sanctioned the **Bay of Pigs** debacle, overseen the **Cuban Missile Crisis**, and committed the United States further into the **Vietnam War**. Ultimately, however, Kennedy is remembered for his untimely departure from office: the victim of an assassin's bullet in 1963. The idea of a youthful, dynamic president, cruelly denied time to achieve his promise, is how many Americans view Kennedy, making him one of the most popular presidents of the twentieth century.

Kennedy, Robert (1925–68) 'Bobby' Kennedy served as the US **Attorney General** and as a close advisor to the administration of his brother, John F. **Kennedy**. Remaining Attorney General for twelve months after his brother's assassination, Kennedy then successfully stood as a **Democratic Party** candidate for the US **Senate**. In 1968, he announced his intention to stand for President of the United States. He had won five out of six of his party's **primary elections** before he too was assassinated. The chain of assassinations at this time – John F. Kennedy (1963), **Malcolm X** (1965), Martin Luther **King** (1968) and Robert Kennedy (1968) – marked some of the most turbulent years for US politics in the twentieth century.

King, Martin Luther (1929–68) A leader of the **civil rights movement** in the United States during the 1950s and 1960s. A Baptist minister, who helped found the Southern Christian Leadership Conference, King called for a non-violent campaign against racial discrimination. He organised a series of protests and boycotts across the south, which culminated in the 'March on Washington' in 1963. He was awarded the Nobel Peace prize a year later. After **Congress** passed the **Civil Rights Act, 1964** and the **Voting Rights, 1965**, King continued to highlight and campaign against racial discrimination both in the north and south of the United States. Latterly, he also began to speak out against the **Vietnam War** and apartheid in South Africa. He was assassinated in 1968, apparently by a white supremacist.

King, Rodney (1965–) An African-American who was arrested for motoring offences by the Los Angeles Police Department (LAPD) in 1991. The arrest, videotaped by a bystander, apparently involved LAPD officers brutally beating King. These images of white policemen beating a black suspect were broadcast nationwide. Charges of assault followed against four LAPD officers, but all were acquitted. News of these acquittals sparked the Los Angeles riots of 1992.

Kissinger, Henry (1923–) A political scientist who served as **National Security Advisor** to the **President**, and then **Secretary of State**, under the administrations of Richard **Nixon** and Gerald **Ford**. Kissinger's major achievements in public office involved developing a diplomatic understanding with both China and the Soviet Union, as well as negotiated settlements in Vietnam and the Middle East.

In terms of Kissinger's Cold War strategy, his policy of *détente* resulted in warmer US relations with China and the Soviet Union. This prompted strategic arms limitation talks (SALT) with Moscow from 1969 onwards, while the early 1970s rapprochement with China represented the first official US contact with the People's Republic since communists had taken power in 1949.

Although he originally advocated a hard-line policy in the **Vietnam War** and helped engineer the US bombing of Cambodia, Kissinger later played a major role in the disengagement of US troops from this country. The ceasefire he negotiated in Paris during 1973 earned Kissinger and his Vietnamese counterpart, Le Duc Tho (who refused the honour), a Nobel Peace prize. This ceasefire, however, did not prevent the fall of South Vietnam to the communist North in 1975. Elsewhere, in the wake of the Arab-Israeli War of 1973, Kissinger used what came to be called 'shuttle diplomacy' in efforts to disengage these opposing armies. As a consequence of brokering these peace talks, Kissinger was responsible for the resumption of diplomatic relations between Egypt and the United States, severed since 1967, which made possible the later **Camp David** Accords.

Despite the above diplomatic successes, Kissinger's reputation has always been dogged by critics pointing to his alleged preference for supporting anti-communist regimes, at the expense of down-playing these regimes' human rights records. Controversy surrounds Kissinger's role in authorising the secret bombing of Cambodia, for example, and backing the 1973 military coup in Chile.

kitchen cabinet Any informal forum of decision makers, effectively rivalling the formal **cabinet**. **President** Ronald **Reagan**, for example, relied upon a 'kitchen cabinet' of friends and acquaintances from California for advice. None of these individuals held public office, but they enjoyed considerable influence.

Ku Klux Klan A secret society intent on securing white supremacy in the United States, often by violent acts. Veterans of the Confederate army originally established the Klan immediately after the **civil war**. Their objective was to resist **reconstruction** and restore old power structures. The Klan was involved in numerous cases of intimidation and violence against newly enfranchised African-Americans. With reconstruction at an end, and segregation largely re-established, the Klan dissolved. A second incarnation of the Ku Klux Klan emerged around 1915, and revolved around a nostalgic yearning for the 'old South'. White citizens of small towns defended their lifestyle against the perceived encroachment of African-American interests (as well as the interests of northerners, Catholics, Jews and 'Bolsheviks'). A burning cross became the symbol of this new organisation, and white-robed Klansmen participated in marches, parades, and night patrols all over the country. Membership of these societies peaked in the 1920s, but fell dramatically during the **Great Depression**. The last major resurfacing of political activity using the name 'Ku Klux Klan' came as a response to the **civil rights movement** in the 1950s and 1960s. 'Klan' members used arson attacks, lynchings and bombings to intimidate African-Americans, and whites from the north, attempting to force them not to join the desegregation campaign. Various scattered organisations claiming allegiance to the Klan still exist today, but they are isolated and politically discredited, numbering only a few thousand members in total.

L

lame duck An ineffective politician, due to changing circumstances. The **President** of the United States, for example, will be a lame duck if they lose their re-election race, as they wait for the new president's inauguration. Similarly, if a **mid-term election** leaves the President with little support in **Congress**, again they will continue weakened, as a 'lame duck'.

layer-cake federalism Another name for **dual federalism**. The analogy refers to the different constituent parts found in a layer-cake. The federal and state governments are distinct and separate, but are both required in order to make up the whole cake/government.

legislative agencies Like the **executive branch**, the federal **legislative branch** also supervises a smaller number of **independent agencies** to help it in its work. These include the **Government Accountability Office**, the Library of **Congress**, and the Government Printing Office.

legislative branch The division of government responsible for making laws. In the case of the US **federal government, Congress** is the sole law-making body. The Congress is divided into two chambers: the **House of Representatives** and the **Senate**. To ensure that each state is equally represented in this body, as are US citizens, each chamber has a different constituency. The Senate comprises of two members from each of the fifty states, irrespective of their total population, while members of the House of Representatives are responsible to 435 constituencies of roughly equal numbers of voters. This system was established by the **Great Compromise** principle negotiated during the drafting of the US **constitution**. Senators and members of the House also have different terms of office: senators sit for six years, while those in the House are elected every two years. As well as undertaking a legislative role, Congress also exercises powers of **oversight**, maintaining **checks and balances**.

Lewinsky, Monica (1973–) A **White House** intern who had an affair with **President** Bill **Clinton**. Revelations of this extra-martial relationship, together with Clinton's initial denial, on oath, of 'sexual relations' with Lewinsky, hampered this politician's second term in office. At a time of aggravation between the **executive branch** and the **legislative branch**, this revelation provided the basis of Articles of **Impeachment** drawn up by the US **House of Representatives** against Clinton. The Senate dismissed these charges. This scandal inevitably goes by the name 'Monica-gate' and 'Zipper-gate'.

limited government Where the work of government is constrained by a higher authority, usually a constitution. All governments in the United States are 'limited' in the sense that none of these can exceed the powers designated to them by the US **constitution**.

Lincoln, Abraham (1809–65) Sixteenth **President** of the United States, holding office between 1861 and 1865. After George **Washington**, Lincoln is perhaps the president still held in most regard by the US people. It was his administration that prosecuted the **civil war**, defeating the rebellious forces of the **Confederate States of America**, and preserving the Union. Lincoln also took the decision to end the practice of slavery in the United States.

Born in Kentucky, and raised in Illinois, Lincoln came from a humble background, working as a shop-keeper, a surveyor, a postal worker, and then a lawyer before entering Illinois state politics in 1834. In 1846, he was elected to the US **House of Representatives** as a member of the **Whig Party**, but only served one term of office. In the 1850s, Lincoln helped reorganise the **Republican Party**, and became this organisation's nominee for President of the United States in 1860. By the time Lincoln arrived in the **White House**, seven southern states had already seceded from the Union.

Lincoln never wavered from his belief that no state had the right to secede from the Union, and that federal laws should be upheld, even if this meant civil war. Similarly, as President, he would not allow the institution of slavery to spread into the new territories of the west. Despite massive casualties on both sides, Lincoln prosecuted the war with determination, granting himself a considerable array of emergency powers. Re-elected to the White House in 1864, Lincoln's last major acts as President were to issue the **Emancipation Proclamation** freeing slaves in the United States, and to advocate leniency for the terms admitting the Confederate states back into the Union. Lincoln was assassinated in April 1865, a few days after his second **inauguration**.

line-item veto The right of a **chief executive** to **veto** a legislative act, not only in its entirety, but also specific individual clauses of a proposal. Parts of an act can thus be removed by veto, leaving the remaining portions intact and legally binding. Most **governors** have the right of line-item veto in the United States, but not the **President** of the United States, who can only veto a Congressional act as a whole. Several presidents have campaigned for an amendment to the **constitution** granting them the right of line-item veto, but this proposal has yet to gain sufficient support. **Congress** did, however, briefly give President Bill **Clinton** this right in 1997, with a simple act of Congress, but this was struck down a year later by the **Supreme Court** in the ruling *Clinton* v. *the City of New York*, 1998.

Little Rock Central High School The scene of a 1957 milestone event in the **civil rights** campaign. **President** Dwight **Eisenhower** deployed federal troops in order to guarantee the safety of nine African-American pupils who wished to attend a newly desegregated school. White protestors had gathered outside the school to prevent these children from entering the school premises, in direct defiance of the **Supreme Court** integration ruling *Brown* v. *Board of Education*, 1954. The political tension surrounding this protest was heightened by the fact that the segregationist Arkansas state **governor**, Orval Faubus, deployed the state national guard to block entry to the school for African-Americans. Eisenhower first federalised the Arkansas National Guard, ordering them to return to barracks, and then replaced them with federal paratroopers, to guarantee order. This was a clear signal that the **federal government** was now prepared to uphold the **constitution** in the southern states, where previously it had tolerated segregationist **Jim Crow laws**.

living constitution A phrase that reflects the idea that a constitution is not set in time and meaning, but can be interpreted differently by different generations to suit their particular needs.

See also: **flexible construction**

log rolling A term referring to an exchange of favours between legislators. A member of **Congress** agreeing to support a colleague pushing through an initiative on agricultural subsidies, in return for reciprocal help winning a separate federal highways project for his or her own state, would be deemed to be 'log rolling'.

Louisiana Purchase An 1803 treaty signed by **President** Thomas **Jefferson** that doubled the territory of the United States. Over five million acres of land were bought from France, which extended the borders of the United States to the Rocky Mountains in the west, and to what is the modern state of Louisiana in the south.

M

McCain-Feingold see **Bipartisan Campaign Reform Act, 2002**

McCarthy, Joseph (1908–57) A **Republican Party** US senator, holding office between 1946 and 1957, who led an anti-communist crusade against public figures. McCarthy first came to the public's attention in 1950 when he claimed that 205 communists had infiltrated the **State Department**. Although he was unable to substantiate this claim, when testifying before the **Senate** Foreign Relations Committee, his campaign gained popularity amidst the general paranoia created at the height of the Cold War. Re-elected to the Senate in 1952, McCarthy was appointed chair of the Committee on Operations, and its investigations sub-committee. He used this position to wage a war against 'un-American activities'. Many public figures were accused of communist affiliations, and brought to testify before his committee. As a consequence of the publicity these hearings generated, individuals lost their jobs or were publicly humiliated, often with little evidence to support the accusations. The phrase 'witch hunt' is often used to describe McCarthy's actions. Eventually, McCarthy's increasingly irresponsible accusations (which even included **President** Dwight **Eisenhower**) and his aggressive public interrogation tactics, began to lose McCarthy public support. When the Republicans lost control of the Senate in 1954, the upper chamber passed a motion of **censure** against McCarthy, reprimanding him for conduct 'contrary to Senate traditions'.

McCarthyism In general terms, to accuse individuals of treachery, and persecute them for their political beliefs, often without proof of guilt. More specifically, this term relates to the activities of Senator Joseph **McCarthy** during the 1950s.

McCulloch v. *Maryland,* **1819** A **Supreme Court** decision that underwrites expansive **federal government** public policy, permitted by the US **constitution's necessary and proper clause**.

In 1816, the US **Congress** passed legislation chartering the Second Bank of the United States, in an effort to stabilise the US national currency. This move proved unpopular in many states. It was viewed as the **federal government** intervening in the jurisdiction of the states. Consequently, Maryland imposed a high rate of taxation on this institution. James McCulloch, the cashier of the Baltimore branch of the Second Bank, refused to pay this tax, and was subsequently sued by the state of Maryland.

Before the Supreme Court, bank officials argued that the state of Maryland was unconstitutionally interfering with a federally chartered institution. The state government, by contrast, asserted that Congress had no authority to impose a federal bank on its territory.

The Court's opinion found in favour of McCulloch. It judged that although the US constitution does not specifically give Congress the right to charter banks, this is permitted by the 'necessary and proper clause'. Congress legitimately passed this legislation to enable it to carry out its **enumerated powers**. The chartering of banks was therefore an **implied power** of Congress under the constitution. This set a precedent justifying an expanded role for the federal government, legitimised by the necessary and proper clause.

Madison, James (1751–1836) **Founding Father**, and fourth **President** of the United States, holding office between 1809 and 1817. Madison was raised on his family's tobacco plantation in Virginia, before becoming a legislator in this state's House of Delegates (1776–9). He also represented Virginia in the **Continental Congress**, and played a leading role in the drafting of the US **constitution**. Defending his work, Madison co-authored the

Federalist Papers, in an effort to persuade the states to ratify this document. As a result of his political skills at the Annapolis and Philadelphia conventions, combined with his successful leadership of the ratification campaign, Americans often refer to Madison as the 'Father of the Constitution'.

Elected to the **House of Representatives** in 1888 for the first session of the US **Congress,** Madison was at the forefront of ratifying the **Bill of Rights** (the first ten amendments of the US constitution). He also acted as **President** George **Washington's floor manager** in the House, and then served in Thomas **Jefferson's** administration as **Secretary of State.** Madison became President himself in 1809, and was re-elected to this office in 1812.

Madison's two administrations were preoccupied with foreign affairs. In particular, the US government had to deal with both France and Great Britain interfering with American merchant shipping. Madison would eventually ask Congress to declare war on Britain. The war of 1812, or 'Madison's War', was a disaster. The US invasion of British Canada failed, and British troops retaliated by burning **Washington DC,** including the new presidential residence: the **White House.** Only British wariness of a repeat of the **War of Independence,** and the distraction of the Napoleonic Wars, ensured that the United States ended this war with its territory still intact.

Majority Leader The title given to the individual elected by colleagues to lead the majority party in a legislative body. The US **Senate** and **House of Representatives,** for example, both have majority leaders. These individuals manage **floor** proceedings on behalf of their party, act as a spokesperson, and attempt to maintain unity amongst party members.

Malcolm X (1925–65) Born Malcolm Little in Nebraska, Malcolm X transformed himself from a small-time crook into one of the most eloquent speakers of the twentieth century addressing the **civil rights** of African-Americans. Malcolm adopted the name 'X' in preference to the surname that had been bestowed upon his forefathers by a slave owner.

Serving eight years in prison for theft and firearms offences, Malcolm joined the Nation of Islam whilst incarcerated, and studied the black nationalist teachings of Elijah Muhammad. This organisation preached that African-Americans should convert to the Muslim faith, and establish their own, separate black nation within the borders of the United States. Only then, it was argued, would white subjugation and exploitation of their black compatriots end. On leaving prison in 1952, Malcolm became a leading organiser within the Nation of Islam, helping to build recognition and the popularity of this movement. Many disaffected African-Americans came to see the idea of a separate black state as the only alternative to the racial exploitation of the *status quo*. The Nation of Islam, in this respect, was a more radical, black nationalist, wing of the broader civil rights campaign of the time.

Malcolm X left the Nation of Islam in 1964, after disagreements with Elijah Muhammed and in-fighting within the organisation's leadership. He established 'Muslim Mosque, Inc.', and later the 'Organization of Afro-American Unity', continuing his fiery anti-racist oratory. Malcolm X was assassinated in 1965, apparently by individuals close to the leadership of the Nation of Islam.

manifest destiny The belief that it was the historical fate of the United States to expand its original territory from the thirteen colonies on the eastern seaboard of America across the whole continent to the Pacific Ocean. This phrase was commonly evoked by advocates of territorial expansion in the nineteenth century, and was even used to justify the United States' brief flirtation with imperialism at the turn of the twentieth century.

marble-cake federalism Another name for **cooperative federalism**. The analogy refers to the different constituent parts found in a marble cake. The federal and state governments are distinct, but are intermingled in order to make up the best example of the cake/government. Another analogy for this style of governing is **picket-fence federalism**.

Marbury v. *Madison*, 1803 The **Supreme Court** decision that established this body's right of constitutional **judicial review**.

The case of *Marbury* v. *Madison* revolved around a political dispute between the administrations of an incoming **President**, Thomas **Jefferson**, and an outgoing one, John Adams. Adams, fearful that Jefferson would undo what the Federalists had achieved in the previous twelve years, appointed over 200 of his party's loyal supporters to **federal government** posts in the last weeks of his presidency. Amongst these appointees was William Marbury, who was to be a Justice of the Peace in **Washington DC**. The dispute arose because the formalities of these appointments were not completed before Jefferson's **inauguration**. Although Marbury's commission had been signed and sealed, it had not been delivered. Angered by the Adams Administration's use of political patronage, the Jefferson Administration refused to complete Marbury's appointment process, along with others left outstanding. Marbury appealed to the Supreme Court.

argued that it was an **implied power** of the constitution. He interlinked three clauses of this document to support his assertion: the constitution states that it is the duty of the judicial branch to interpret the laws of the land; similarly, it declares that the constitution is the supreme law of the United States; and it also requires court officials to swear to uphold the constitution. Thus, Marshall's logic was, courts are established to interpret laws. It therefore follows that they have authority to judge cases involving the law of the constitution. Faced with two laws, one made by Congress, and the other the constitution itself, courts are duty bound to recognise the supremacy of the latter. It is therefore the Supreme Court's duty to uphold the constitution by striking down any conflicting law, making it null and void.

From this point onwards, with the power of judicial review, the Supreme Court developed into an important arbiter between citizens and their government, and between the institutions of government. By the end of the civil war (1861–5), Marshall's logic, espoused in *Marbury* v. *Madison*, had become fully accepted within the US political system.

Marine One Marine Helicopter Squadron One is dedicated to providing helicopter transport for the **President** and presidential staff on official business. 'Marine One' is the radio call-sign used to identify a helicopter when the President is on board.

mark-up The final Congressional committee session, where a bill is fine-tuned before being proposed to the **floor** of the **House of Representatives** or **Senate**.

Mason–Dixon line In modern usage, an imaginary line that separates the northern and southern states of the USA, symbolically emphasising the different cultural, social, economic and political traditions of these two regions. The original Mason–Dixon line, named after the two British surveyors who demarcated this territory in the 1760s, was drawn to define the disputed border between colonial Pennsylvania and Maryland.

Medicaid A national social security programme providing health insurance for those individuals on a low income and under the age of 65, as well as those over this age who have exhausted their **Medicare** entitlement. Medicaid came into operation in 1966 as part of **President** Lyndon B. **Johnson**'s **Great Society** reforms. The **federal government** funds between 50 and 80 per cent of the costs of this programme, with state governments contributing the balance. Qualification for this benefit is determined by local state legislation (and restrictions subsequently enacted by **Congress**), but the federal government requires all who receive public welfare assistance to be covered by this scheme.

Medicare A national social security programme providing health insurance for US citizens aged 65 years or over. There are restrictions on the length of time an individual is entitled to receive Medicaid, as well as the number of times a person may apply for this assistance. This scheme came into operation in 1966 as part of **President** Lyndon B. **Johnson**'s **Great Society** reforms, and is funded by the **federal government**.
Website: http://www.medicare.gov

mid-term elections Federal **general election**s are scheduled every two years, when all seats of the **House of Representatives** are contested, along with one-third of the **Senate**'s membership. 'Mid-terms' are those elections that fall in a non-presidential-race year. In this respect, 2008 will be a presidential year, 2010 will be a mid-term election year, 2012 will be another presidential year, 2014 will be a mid-term year, and so on.

military–industrial complex A term coined by **President** Dwight D. **Eisenhower**, highlighting the three-way relationship between commercial interests (mainly defence contractors), politicians (both legislators and members of the **executive branch**), and the armed forces of the United States. It is argued that all constituents within this **iron triangle** benefit from the growth of the military and its acquisition of new and better weapons systems. The danger of the military–industrial complex is that such an expansion of military might is not necessarily the best way for the US to spend its resources, and may lead to an aggressive foreign policy.

minority leader The title given to the individual elected by members of the second largest party in a chamber who leads the opposition in US legislative bodies. The US **Senate** and **House of Representatives**, for example, both have minority leaders. These individuals manage **floor** proceedings on behalf of the opposition, act as a spokesperson, and attempt to maintain unity amongst party members.

minority president There are two definitions of a minority **President**. In the first category are those **chief executives** who, although they are legitimately elected, gained fewer popular votes than their opponents. This is possible due to the mechanism of the **electoral college**. An alternative definition is a President who polled less than 50 per cent of the total popular vote. This can occur when there are more than two candidates standing.

Miranda v. *Arizona*, 1966 A **Supreme Court** decision that underpins the rights of those who are suspected of criminal acts in the United States. In 1963, Ernesto Miranda was arrested near Phoenix, Arizona, and charged with kidnapping and rape. After being identified by the victim, and being interrogated by police officers for two hours, he confessed to these crimes. Miranda was subsequently convicted on the basis of this confession, and received a custodial sentence. Key to this individual's subsequent appeal was the fact that at no time during this police interrogation was Miranda advised of his right to silence and legal counsel. Miranda's appeal lawyer therefore argued that his client's rights under the **Fifth Amendment** to the US **constitution** had been violated.

Despite the state of Arizona counter-arguing that Miranda could have asked for legal representation at any time during his interrogation, and that nobody had forced him to confess to these crimes, the Supreme Court decided that the state had not sufficiently protected Miranda's constitutional rights. His conviction was quashed. Consequently, law informant agencies now inform those they arrest of their 'Miranda rights': suspects have the right to remain silent; anything said may be used in a court of law; all accused have the right to legal representation; and that legal representation will be provided free of charge if the accused cannot afford to employ their own counsel.

Missouri compromise An 1820–1 Congressional agreement that saw the territories of Missouri and Maine become states of the Union, the former as a 'slave state', and the latter as a 'free state'. It was also decided, with any other future states joining the Union, that slave holding would only be permitted in territories below the 36th parallel. With the power of slave states and free states evenly balanced in the first half of the nineteenth century, neither side wished to see any of the new states being carved out of the western frontier upset this north–south political equilibrium, hence the compromise, and a maintenance of the balance of power. The Missouri compromise endured until the US **Congress** passed the Kansas-Nebraska Act of 1854, which potentially permitted both these territories be admitted to the Union as 'slave states', even though they were both located above the 36th parallel. With the willingness to compromise now diminished in Congress, this 1854 act was a significant step on the road to **civil war**.

modern presidency Reference to a presidential era evolving since the 1930s, where the **chief executive** has been willing to place the **White House** at the heart of legislative programmes tackling national social and economic issues (Franklin D. **Roosevelt's New Deal,** for example, or Lyndon B. **Johnson's Great Society** reforms). Similarly, 'modern **Presidents**' have used their constitutional powers in the field of foreign and military affairs more widely, projecting US power abroad (including Roosevelt entering World War Two, and subsequent Presidents' prosecution of the Cold War). Modern Presidents have also appealed directly to the people using new forms of media technology, rather than relying on the traditional channel of communication though the people's representatives in **Congress** (Roosevelt's radio **fireside chats,** for instance, or Ronald **Reagan's** use of television). This era of the US presidency is distinct from the earlier period of the **traditional presidency**.

Monica-gate see **Lewinsky, Monica**

Monroe Doctrine A proclamation made by **President** James Monroe in 1823, indicating that the United States would regard as hostile any further attempt by a European power to establish a colony in the Americas, or, likewise, to interfere with the affairs of any sovereign state on this continent. In return, the United States pledged to remain neutral in disputes between European states.

Montesquieu, Baron de (1689–1755) Charles-Louis de Secondat, Baron de La Brède et de Montesquieu, was a French political philosopher, whose ideas of a **separation of the powers** and **checks and balances** between branches of government were later adopted by the **Founding Fathers** when drafting the US **constitution**. His key work was the *De l'esprit des lois* (*The Spirit of the Laws*) published in 1748.

Montgomery bus boycott A 1955–6 political protest by African-Americans against racial discrimination on the public transit system of Montgomery, Alabama. After Rosa Parks was arrested in December 1955 for refusing to give up her bus seat for a fellow white passenger, a boycott of this city's public transit system ensued. This was managed by a **civil rights** organisation led by Martin Luther **King**. The boycott proved successful, and in 1956, the discriminatory policies of the city's bus company were ruled unconstitutional by the US **Supreme Court**. The Montgomery bus boycott gave the **civil rights movement** one of its first major victories, and brought King to the attention of the nation.

moral majority see **Christian Right**

Motor-Voter Act An epithet for the National Voter Registration Act passed by the US **Congress** in 1993. Aiming to increase the number of US citizens registering for, and subsequently participating in, federal elections, this act makes it possible for individuals to register to vote in a wide range of federal buildings, not just via electoral offices, as had been the case previously. The act also simplified the registration process. It was dubbed the 'motor-voter' act as some of the new offices processing registration forms were federal drivers' licence centres.

Website: http://www.motorvoter.com/motorhome.htm

N

NAACP see **National Association for the Advancement of Colored People**

Nader, Ralph (1934–) A political activist on the Left of US politics, championing environmental issues, democratic rights and consumer protection. He has stood as a presidential candidate on several occasions, both as an independent and representing the Green Party.

NAFTA see **North American Free Trade Agreement**

National Association for the Advancement of Colored People
An interest group formed in 1909 to protect and expand the **civil rights** of African-Americans. For almost a century, the NAACP has mounted numerous legal challenges to discriminatory laws and practices in the United States. NAACP legal counsel, for example, prosecuted the case of *Brown* v. *Board of Education*, 1954. This organisation also played a leadership role during the 1950s and 1960s, at the height of the civil rights campaign. Today, the NAACP continues its work rooting out racism in the United States, highlighting areas of dis-

crimination, and lobbying and speaking out on issues pertinent to the African-American community.

Website: http://www.naacp.org

national debt The sum the government of the United States owes it creditors. Most western governments have a national debt. However, the **federal government** from the 1970s onwards ran a series of **budget deficits** that eventually created considerable political concern over the size of the US national debt. **Congress** responded to this perceived crisis by passing a series of acts. The Balanced Budget and Emergency Deficit Control Act, 1985 (also known as Gramm-Rudman-Hollings after its sponsors), for example, dictated specific deficit targets for future budgets, and established a sequestration procedure to reduce spending if those sums were exceeded. The Budget Enforcement Act, 1990 extended these targets. A number of budget surpluses were recorded as a result of this legislation. Once the provisions of the Budget Enforcement Act expired, however, **President** George W. **Bush** presided over a series of tax cuts that once more created deficits and increased the national debt. There have been several attempts over recent years to pass a **constitutional amendment** requiring the **executive branch** to maintain a balanced budget.

National Governors Association An organisation that brings together all the **governors** of the fifty states, and those of the US territories (American Samoa, Guam, the Northern Mariana Islands, Puerto Rico, and the US Virgin Islands). As well as providing a forum of networking for these leaders, the National Governors Association collectively lobbies the **federal government** on state (and territory) issues, and develops public policy and best practice relevant to the states.

Website: http://www.nga.org/portal/site/nga

national guard The United States National Guard is the reserve force of the US military. It comprises regular units, and, additionally, state militias. The state militias are under the command of their respective state **governor**s, and are deployed locally to assist in emergencies (forest fires or flooding, for instance), and to maintain law and order (to quell civil disobedience, such as rioting). These militias are, however, fully trained and combat ready. Should the need arise, these troops may be 'federalised' by command of the **President** of the United States and deployed on **federal government** missions. Federal duties have precedence over state needs, and 'federalisation' is permissible even without the relevant state governor's permission (see **Little Rock Central High School**).

Websites: http://www.arng.army.mil and http://www.ang.af.mil

national party convention Where delegates of a political party meet every four years to select a candidate to stand for **President** of the United States. These conventions also provide a forum where the national party **platform** is finalised, outlining principles and polices for the forthcoming elections. As, in more modern times, the party's presidential nominee is now decided by **primary elections**, the national convention has taken on a more ceremonial role. The winner of the primary contest is confirmed amongst shows of party unity and jubilation, and the publicity generated by this event is used to launch the party's campaign for the **general election** in November. In the past, national conventions were less stage-managed. They were arenas where political deals were struck. Amongst this political bargaining, who would actually receive the party's nomination for president often remained in doubt until the final ballot had taken place.

National Rifle Association Established in 1871, the NRA is a powerful interest group representing gun owners in the United States. Politically, it is very active in lobbying against gun-control legislation. Controversy surrounds this area of public policy, as a result of the country's high levels of gun crime conflicting with the apparent right of Americans to own weapons under the **Second Amendment** to the US **constitution**.

Website: http://www.nra.org

National Security Advisor The Assistant to the President for National Security Affairs serves as the **chief executive's** prime advisor on national security, and administers the **National Security Council**. This individual is independent of the Departments of State and Defense, and is not subject to **Senate** confirmation before being appointed.

National Security Council The NSC is a unit of the **executive branch** established to assist the **President** in making and executing national security decisions. Along with the President attending, the Council gathers together the **Vice President**, the **Secretary of State**, the Secretary of the Treasury, the Secretary of Defense, and the Assistant to the President for National Security Affairs (commonly referred to as the **National Security Advisor**). The Chairman of the **Joint Chiefs of Staff** is the statutory military advisor to the Council, and the Director of the Central Intelligence Agency is the intelligence advisor. The **Chief of Staff** to the President, Counsel to the President, and the Assistant to the President for Economic Policy are invited to attend all NSC meetings. The **Attorney General** and the Director of the **Office of Management and Budget** are invited to attend meetings pertaining to their responsibilities. The heads of other executive departments and agencies, as well as other senior officials, are also occasionally part of the NSC's deliberations, when appropriate.

Established in 1947, the NSC has no formal powers, takes no votes, and makes no decisions of its own. The Council's work merely serves to help the President make an informed decision. The President will often consult members of the NSC individually, or in smaller groups, avoiding holding a full meeting of this body.

Website: http://www.whitehouse.gov/nsc

National Voter Registration Act, 1993 see **Motor-Voter Act**

necessary and proper clause see **implied powers**

negative campaigning When a candidate seeks to win an election by attacking his or her opponent's character and policies, rather than emphasising the positives they themselves could potentially contribute to this office.

neocon see **neo-conservative**

neo-conservative An ill-defined term, more frequently used in the 1990s and twenty-first century to describe individuals broadly subscribing to the views of the **New Right** and **Christian Right**. Neo-conservatives of the modern era are more likely to sanction foreign policy intervention, to spread 'liberty' and 'democracy' abroad, than previous generations of US conservatives.

New Deal A broad programme of public policy implemented during the presidency of Franklin D. **Roosevelt** designed to counter the effects of the **Great Depression**. Roosevelt's comprehensive set of measures included banking reforms, economic regeneration initiatives, public works schemes, welfare reforms and labour legislation. Although the New Deal was successful in helping many Americans cope with the harsh economic and social conditions of the 1930s, whether this programme was a success strategically is still debated by historians. Ultimately, US fortunes would only recover with the economic stimulation created by the Second World War. A major legacy of the New Deal was the **federal government**'s new willingness to intervene, in an effort to guarantee minimum national social and economic standards.

New Deal coalition An alignment of politicians, interest groups and voters which first coalesced around Franklin D. **Roosevelt**'s **New Deal** in the 1930s. This coalition then continued to back the **Democratic Party** during the 1940s, 1950s and 1960s, supporting this party's social and economic reforms. The main constituent parts of the New Deal coalition were the Democratic Party itself, labour unions, and minority groups. The coalition dissolved during the 1960s due to rifts created by the **civil rights movement**, the **Vietnam War** and **affirmative action**.

new federalism Reference to a movement in US politics, popular since the 1970s, aiming to restore political power to the states. New federalists believe that Washington DC has gained too much of an upper hand with respect to the state/federal balance since the implementation of the **New Deal** in the 1930s, and particularly in more recent times. One tool of the new federalism has been to grant federal **block grants** to the states. These budgets give local governments considerable autonomy over how money is spent, rather than the more traditional **categorical grants**, where the **federal government** directed how states should use this aid.

New Frontier Reference to **President** John F. **Kennedy's** legislative programme that established the US Peace Corps, urban regeneration projects, and welfare reforms. Kennedy suffered defeats on many of his proposed bills. His successor, President Lyndon B. **Johnson,** achieved more success with his **Great Society** reforms. The term 'New Frontier' is drawn from Kennedy's **nomination** acceptance speech where he stated: 'We stand today on the edge of a new frontier – the frontier of the 1960s, a frontier of unknown opportunities and paths.'

New Right In terms of US party politics, the term New Right is used to refer to a movement within the **Republican Party** that gained momentum during the 1960s and 1970s, which successfully built a new electoral apparatus and advocated competitive policies. This New Right activism helped end the **Democratic Party's** domination of US politics stemming from the era of the **New Deal coalition** (1930s to 1960s). Republican victories came with first Richard **Nixon** being elected president in 1969, followed by Ronald **Reagan's** two administrations in the 1980s, and then Presidents Bush senior and junior. The Republican Party has also enjoyed a resurgence of its electoral fortunes in the US **Congress** during this same period.

Ideologically, the New Right movement is broader than just the organisational capacity of the Republican Party. Indeed, the neo-liberal economic principles of this school of thought came to influence many western governments from the 1970s onwards. In the US context, ideologically, New Right ideas have been taken up by the **Christian Right** and other **neo-conservatives**.

9/11 Reference to the date of 11 September 2001, when two passenger planes were hi-jacked by al-Qa'ida operatives and deliberately crashed into the twin towers of the World Trade Center in New York City. Another hijacked plane hit the **Pentagon,** while a fourth failed to reach its intended target. These acts prompted, by way of response, **President** George W. **Bush's** 'War on Terror'.

Nixon, Richard (1913–94) Thirty-seventh **President** of the United States, holding office between 1969 and 1974. Richard Milhous Nixon, raised in California, served in the United States Navy during the Second World War, before being elected to the US **House of Representatives** as a Republican in 1946. In 1950, he became a US senator for the state of California, and between 1953 and 1961 served as President Dwight **Eisenhower's Vice President.** Only the narrowest of margins, in the popular vote of 1960, saw Nixon lose to John F. **Kennedy** for the presidency of the United States. He spent the next few years in political semi-retirement, before winning the 1968 **White House** race, and was re-elected President of the United States in 1972.

Although criticised for his style of leadership (see **imperial president**), Nixon achieved considerable feats in foreign affairs during his time as **chief executive.** He extricated US forces from the **Vietnam War,** and negotiated treaties with the communist powers of the Soviet Union and China. Domestically, he also successfully created two new executive agencies, in the fields of the environment, and health and safety, and developed federal social security policy. Overshadowing all these achievements, however, is the **Watergate** scandal. Nixon, accused of trying to cover up the politically motivated burglary of a **Democratic National Committee** office, and **impeached** by the House of Representatives, became the only President to resign from office in US history.

nomination The act of proposing a candidate for public office. Candidates seeking election for **President** of the United States, for example, are nominated at their respective **national party conventions**. Delegates from this party, representing all the states, come together every four years to decide who will be their candidate for the forthcoming elections. Previously, the nomination conventions involved a good deal of 'horse trading' amongst different sets of supporters within the party. Today, **primary elections**, held prior to the convention, determine who will receive the party's backing.

Nominations are also required as part of the process determining who will staff the upper echelons of the **executive branch** (the Secretary to the Treasury, for example, or a US ambassador to a foreign country). In the case of the **federal government,** the President will nominate the individual they wish to serve under them. It is then up to the Senate to approve this appointment, or not, through **confirmation hearings.**

North American Free Trade Agreement NAFTA is a treaty of economic cooperation, signed by the United States, Canada and Mexico. Operating since 1994, this agreement has seen a reduction of trade tariffs between these three countries. NAFTA also encompasses agreement on a number of minimum environmental standards. Unlike the European Union, this treaty created no supranational institutions.

North, Oliver (1943–) Colonel Oliver North, a US Marine assigned to the **National Security Council** staff during the administration of **President** Ronald **Reagan,** came to the public's attention during the **Irangate** scandal of the 1980s. He was one of the key managers of the arms-for-hostages deal. He received a three-year suspended prison sentence for attempting to obstruct the investigation of this scandal, which was later overturned in 1991 (as prosecution evidence, the judge agreed, was influenced by North's Congressional testimony, for which he had received partial immunity). Due to his passionate performance during the Irangate hearings, North became a doyen of the **Christian Right,** and ran (unsuccessfully) for the US **Senate.** Today, North is a neo-conservative media commentator.

NRA see **National Rifle Association**

NSC see **National Security Council**

O

Office of Management and Budget The OMB, established in 1921, is a division of the **executive branch** that is charged with assisting the **President** formulate the proposed annual federal budget. Once Congress has agreed a budget, it is also the OMB's duty to manage this legislation, allocating executive departments and agencies tranches of money on a periodic basis.

Website: http://www.whitehouse.gov/omb

OMB see **Office of Management and Budget**

omnibus bill Where several items of proposed legislation, often largely unrelated, are considered together in one single large bill. These items are usually debated together in order to assist the time management of a legislative body. The US **Congress,** for example, often approves the federal budget via an omnibus bill.

open primary Where voters have a choice of which party's **primary election** they wish to participate in. Given the dominance of the **two-party system**, when entering a polling station, voters will usually either select a ballot relating to **Republican Party** hopefuls, or one relating to **Democratic Party** contenders. By contrast, in a **closed primary**, voters may only participate in a ballot if they have registered their affiliation to that party prior to election day.

opinion of the Supreme Court The 'opinion' of the **Supreme Court** is a written document, authored by a justice supporting the majority view, outlining the Court's decision in a case. This document explains the legal reasoning behind the verdict. Such opinions have had dramatic consequences for US politics and society over the years. *Brown* v. *Board of Education*, **1954**, for example, outlawed segregation, while *United States* v. *Nixon*, **1974** led to the resignation of a **President**. In addition to 'the' opinion in a Supreme Court case, there may also be other, minority, opinions. **Concurring opinions** are written by one or more justices who support the overall decision of the Court, but differ from, or wish to add to, the legal reasoning behind 'the' opinion, while a **dissenting opinion** (or opinions) will be written by justices who disagree with the actual verdict itself.

originalist see **strict construction**

Oval Office The name given to the President's official office in the **White House**, so called because of its shape.

oversight The process of one institution or branch of government supervising and inspecting the work of another. Such scrutiny is at the heart of the United States system of **checks and balances**.

P

PAC see **political action committee**

Parks, Rosa (1913–2005) see **Montgomery bus boycott**

pardon The removal of the legal consequences of a crime or conviction. The **President** has the constitutional authority (Article Two, Section Two) to pardon any individual who has committed a crime or other offence against the United States. This power was included in the US **constitution** by the **Founding Fathers** to provide a **check and balance** on the **judicial branch** of government, and to facilitate reconciliation after rebellion. Most famously, **President** Gerald **Ford** granted Richard **Nixon** a pardon in 1974 for any crimes that may have been committed during the **Watergate** scandal. The only conviction the President may not pardon is an **impeachment** verdict. Most state constitutions grant similar pardon powers to respective state **governors**, enabling them to pardon those convicted of state crimes.

parochialism Literally, acting with a narrowness of scope, concentrating on the local. Members of the US **Congress** are often accused of being parochial. This is because they dedicate much of their energy to serving their constituents, or particular interests associated with their own state or district. Although parochialism may be applauded, given that it bolsters democratic representation, it often hinders governance at the national level. With so many members of Congress concentrating on their constituency needs, sometimes the broader *national* interest suffers.

partisan Strong, unreasoned affiliation to a political party or cause. The US **Congress**, for example, is said to divide along partisan lines when members vote with their party, serving party interests, rather than considering an issue on its individual merits.

party convention see **national party convention**

party decline Reference to the fact that US citizens are today more likely to regard themselves, and behave, as 'independent voters', rather than being affiliated to a specific political party. Whereas before, up until the 1950s and 1960s, it was relatively easy to find 'life-long' **Democratic Party** or **Republican Party** supporters, in more modern times, many of the electorate regularly change their political allegiance. Instances of **split-ticket voting** have also increased. Various explanations for party 'decline' have been offered, amongst them the rise of the **candidate-centred election**, competition from interest groups, and the Democratic Party's alienation of southern voters during the second half of the twentieth century. However, although clearly relevant, the 'party in decline thesis' may be taken too far. Voting blocks of citizens (minorities, business interests, union members, and so on), as a whole, may still be identified as being affiliated to either the Republicans or Democrats, and these two parties still dominate the staffing and functions of government at all political levels in the United States.

party nomination see **nomination**

party platform see **platform**

patronage see **appointment power**

Peace Corps Volunteers, managed by an agency of the **federal government**, who share their skills and experience, assisting development projects in the Third World. **President John F. Kennedy** established this agency in 1961, as part of his **New Frontier** initiatives.

Pentagon Literally, the five-sided building located outside **Washington DC** that is the headquarters of the US Department of Defense. The phrase 'the Pentagon' is often used as a synonym for this institution of the **federal government**.

Perot, Ross (1930–) A contender in the 1992 and 1996 presidential elections, standing initially as an independent and then as a third-party candidate. Perot, a multi-millionaire businessman from Texas, campaigned largely on one issue, balancing the federal budget. Disillusioned with the two major parties' handling of this problem, and 'big-government' in general, Perot self-financed these two presidential races, as well as establishing the **Reform Party** in 1995. Running a simple but effective 'anti-Washington DC' campaign, Perot gained considerable success in the 1992 election (taking 19 per cent of the popular vote), but was less successful in 1996 (winning 8 per cent).

picket-fence federalism Another term for **cooperative federalism**, where national and state institutions govern together in partnership, as opposed to **dual federalism**, where each division of government only concerns itself with its own distinct and separate jurisdiction. The picket-fence analogy places national, state, and local governments as the horizontal supports of a fence of vertical pickets that represent different policies. Each horizontal level of government works together to develop the policy represented by the picket. By cooperating, these levels of government are best placed to support/serve the whole fence/society. Another analogy for this style of governing is **marble-cake federalism**.

platform A manifesto of principles and policies that a candidate or party seeks to be elected upon. Although important, US political platforms tend to be less detailed and binding than the equivalent manifestos of European parties.

Plessy v. *Ferguson*, **1896** A **Supreme Court** decision that sanctioned racial discrimination in the United States, as long as each group was treated 'separately but equal'. Despite the **civil war**, and the subsequent ratification of the **thirteenth** and Fourteenth Amendments, discriminatory **Jim Crow laws** returned rapidly to the southern states. In 1890, Homer Plessy, on behalf of a citizens' group, bought a first-class rail ticket to travel in the state of Louisiana. On boarding the train, he informed the conductor of his racial origin (one-eighth African-American). When asked to move to the 'colored' carriage, Plessy refused, and was subsequently arrested. The Supreme Court was asked to judge whether the Louisiana state law requiring railway companies to provide separate 'white' and 'colored' travelling accommodation violated Plessy's rights under the Thirteenth and Fourteenth Amendments to the US **constitution**.

The Court ruled that Plessy's rights had not been abridged. The **opinion** reasoned that as long as citizens from different races were given equal provision (in this instance, a similar standard of railway-carriage accommodation), then this provision could be separate. State governments in the south used *Plessy* v. *Ferguson* as a precedent to legally separate the races in public places, and to discriminate in their public policy. In most cases, the 'equality' element of this 'separate but equal' provision failed to materialise. Discrimination in the southern states continued until outlawed by a subsequent Supreme Court decision *Brown* v. *Board of Education*, 1954, which overturned *Plessy* v. *Ferguson*.

pocket veto Where the **President** blocks a legislative bill via inaction, failing to process it within ten days of a Congressional recess. In the normal course of events, the President will either sign a bill into law or return it to **Congress** with a **veto** message. One of these two options must be taken within ten days, or the bill automatically becomes law. However, if a Congressional session ends within ten days of a bill being sent to the **White House**, then the President is under no obligation to do anything. He or she may choose to act or not. In the latter case, the bill becomes null and void, having run out of time. It is called a pocket veto, as the President simply disregards the issue, and 'puts the bill in his pocket', knowing that the normal ten-day time limit cannot apply.

political action committee PACs are the means through which organisations (such as corporations, labour unions and interest groups) donate money to political campaigns. These committees register with the **Federal Election Commission**, and may donate up to US$5,000 to any one candidate per election, and up to US$15,000 to any one political party per annum. PACs have grown in number since **campaign finance reform** legislation in the 1970s, and serve as a tool for organisations to donate money in a transparent and legal manner. PAC donations, however, become more controversial when this money is used for negative campaigning.

See also: **527 groups**

Populist Party A third party, supported by agricultural workers and farmers, which emerged in the late nineteenth century, protesting against the **federal government**'s monetary policy.

pork barrel politics Pork barrel politics is when the legislative motive of a representative is primarily about securing funding for their own constituency. This **parochial** approach may be at the expense of the collective or national good. In the case of a military programme 'pork barrel', for example, members of **Congress** may prioritise trying to win a defence contract for a business in their own constituency, rather than take a wider, national, view of where best this contract may be placed. The term 'pork barrel' comes from a practice on pre-**civil war** plantations, where slaves received food via dipping their hands into barrels of salted pork. Similarly, politicians seek to 'bring home the bacon' to their own constituencies.

precinct The lowest constituency division found in the United States. These areas are used for the administration of elections, similar to 'wards' in British politics. Major political parties often employ a 'precinct captain' to campaign locally on this organisation's behalf, as well as providing feedback on the political views of the residents of this area.

pre-emption, federal see **federal pre-emption**

President The US **constitution** vests all executive power of the **federal government** in one individual, the President of the United States. He, not yet she, is head of state, and is responsible for implementing Congressional legislation. This office derives specific powers from the constitution, such as being **Commander in Chief** of US military forces. The President also negotiates treaties on behalf of the United States, and appoints ambassadors. Informally, the President gains additional political influence from being the leading figure in the ruling party, and through his powers of **patronage**. Assisting him are some four million civilian and military personnel that make up the **executive branch**. The above powers should, however, be seen in the context of the constitution's system of **checks and balances**.

The US President serves a fixed term of four years' duration, and, since the ratification of the **Twenty-second Amendment** to the constitution in 1951, may only be elected to this office twice. To win the **White House**, presidential candidates need to perform well in **primary elections**, gain their party's **nomination**, and then post a majority of votes in the **electoral college** after a nationwide poll. The President and the **Vice President** are the only politicians in the United States that are elected by, and serve, a single national constituency.

Historically, the President played a supporting role to the US **Congress**. The office was more an administrative post, making sure federal laws and polices were implemented. With the advent of the **modern presidency**, however, from the 1930s onwards, the **chief executive** has taken on more of a leadership role, most often *initiating* national policy. The President has come to personify the federal government. Some commentators argue that Presidents simply do not have enough power at their disposal to fulfil this role. This has led more recent chief executives to occasionally over-extend their reach, becoming **imperial presidents**. Ultimately, as Richard Neustadt points out, successful modern presidents have to rely on their power to persuade others, building coalitions of support, rather than relying on their limited constitutional powers.

Further reading: Richard E. Neustadt, *Presidential Power and the Modern Presidents: The Politics of Leadership from Roosevelt to Reagan* (New York: Free Press, 1991)

Website: http://www.whitehouse.gov

president pro tempore of the Senate Literally translated from the Latin: president 'for the time being'. The US **constitution** states that the US **Vice President** is the presiding officer of the US **Senate**. Vice Presidents have not undertaken this role, on a day-to-day basis, since the very first sessions of **Congress**. They tend now only to attend Congress for ceremonial duties or to break a tie in a Senate vote. In their absence, the chamber elects a president pro tempore. This individual, inevitably from the majority party, acts as a 'speaker' for the Senate, and is third in line in the order of **presidential succession**.

presidential succession Should the President of the United States die in office, resign from this post, or be removed by the **impeachment process**, the US **constitution** directs that the **Vice President** should assume these powers for the remainder of the current term of office. The **Twenty-fifth Amendment** to this constitution, ratified in 1967, confirms that the Vice President becomes President, and not just an Acting President, under these circumstances. This amendment also outlines the procedure to be taken if the President is temporarily unable to carry out his or her duties (the Vice President becomes Acting President until the President communicates to **Congress** that he or she is able to resume office).

Congressional legislation has been enacted to settle the succession issue should both the offices of the President and Vice President become vacant at the same time.

Currently, the **president pro tempore of the Senate** and the **Speaker of the House** are next in line to the White House, followed by a number of **cabinet** members listed in order (from the **Secretary of State** through to the Secretary of Veterans' Affairs).

primary election A poll that ultimately decides which contestant will stand as a party's official candidate in an election. For example, in a presidential election year, both the **Republican Party** and the **Democratic Party** will hold a series of parallel presidential primaries in different states across the country. The objective, in each case, is to select just one individual from a number of presidential hopefuls. The winner of these primaries will receive their respective party's **nomination**, becoming this party's official candidate for **President** in the forthcoming November **general election**. Primaries have the effect of narrowing down a field of several contenders within one party to just one candidate per party.

Two important characteristics of the primary system result from who actually votes in these elections, and the indirect nature of these polls. In the former case, the voters in primaries are the electorate itself. Unlike European political parties, where candidates are selected by party leaders, or by these organisations' membership, with US primaries, 'ordinary' citizens participate in selecting party candidates. Each state has its own electoral law with respect to primaries (see, for example, **open primary** and **closed primary**), but in all cases, it is the general public that decides who they wish to see go forward as this party's candidate for the November elections. In this respect, US voters get two bites of the cherry. They first participate in selecting one individual from a party's potential candidates (primaries). They then have the opportunity to choose between the parties themselves (the November general election).

The second important characteristic is the indirect nature of these polls. Instead of actually voting for a preferred choice of candidate, primary voters are instead choosing who will attend this party's **national convention** as a delegate. It is the delegates at this event who actually decide which candidate will receive their party's nomination. In the past, delegates operated with a degree of independence at the conventions, and could decide themselves who they wished to back for the nomination. Today, in most states, delegates declare in advance whom they will support, so electors can be sure they are selecting the right delegate to attend the national convention.

power of appointment see **appointment power**

pro-choice movement Those who support the legal right of abortion in the United States. The term 'pro-choice' is used as this movement believes a woman has the right to choose on issues relating to her body.

Progressive Party A political party established by Theodore **Roosevelt** to contest the 1912 presidential election. Roosevelt took this action after a dispute with the leadership of the **Republican Party**. With the Republican vote split, Woodrow **Wilson**, the **Democratic Party** candidate, was elected to the **White House**, and the Progressive Party soon disbanded, with Roosevelt returning to the Republican fold.

prohibition Reference to a period of US history where the manufacture and sale of alcoholic beverages was made illegal nationwide. This ban was imposed by the

Eighteenth Amendment to the US **constitution**, ratified in 1919, and ended with the Twenty-first Amendment of 1933.

pro-life movement Those who are against abortion. The term has also expanded to describe those who oppose euthanasia, human cloning and embryonic human stem-cell research.

Publius The pseudonym used by James **Madison,** Alexander **Hamilton** and John Jay when writing the **Federalist Papers.**

Q

Quorum The required number of members of a committee or chamber that must be present to make this body's business valid. The quorum of both the US **Senate** and **House of Representatives** is half its membership, plus one. However, these chambers often operate with less than this number, as by convention it is assumed that there is a quorum unless this assumption is challenged. Members may make such a challenge in order to disrupt proceedings, or to create time for a legislative compromise or other deal to be negotiated. The challenge triggers a **roll call** of members.

R

radical reconstruction see **reconstruction**

ratification Where one institution or body confirms a proposal made by another, as part of a formal decision-making process. It was agreed, for example, that the US **constitution**, authored by delegates at a convention, needed to be ratified by at least nine of the thirteen states of the Union before it became binding for any of them. Similarly, any amendments to this constitution require agreement between the US **Congress** and the states. The states ratify a proposal made by Congress, or *vice versa*.

Reagan democrats Traditional Democratic Party voters and politicians who, across party lines, supported the policies of Ronald Reagan in the 1980s.

See also: **Blue Dog Democrats**

Reagan, Ronald (1911–2004) Fortieth **President** of the United States, holding office between 1981 and 1989. Reagan was raised in Illinois, before building an acting career in Hollywood, California. Starring as the leading man in several 'B-movies' and numerous television dramas, Reagan's acting career lasted for almost thirty years. During this time he served as the president of the Screen Actors Guild, and his political allegiance shifted from the **Democratic Party** to the **Republican Party**. In 1966 he successfully campaigned to be a Republican **Governor** of California, and was re-elected in 1970. After two prior bids to become **President** of the United States (1968 and 1976), Reagan arrived in the **White House** in 1981.

Reagan's two administrations can be characterised by neo-liberal economics in domestic policy, and anti-communism in foreign affairs. Reagan's domestic programme revolved around 'Reagonomics'. Tax cuts were implemented, combined with cost-cutting in federal spending. The US economy recovered during the 1980s, but debate still continues as to whether this was a consequence of Reagan's policies or despite them. One area exempt from this tightening of public spending was defence (increasing the national debt significantly). Reagan dramatically enlarged the military capability of the United States, taking a confrontational stance towards the Soviet Union, and any state deemed to be an ally of what Reagan termed 'the evil empire'. This approach eventually brought the Soviet Union to the negotiating table, and Reagan's supporters claim that this precipitated the end of the Cold War. Detractors point to the human cost resulting from the number of right-wing authoritarian states the Reagan Administration backed as part of its anti-communist foreign policy. The **Irangate** scandal can be seen as a consequence of this stance. Despite these issues, in the United States itself, Reagan is remembered with much affection, due to his overtly patriotic demeanour, combined with his skills as a political communicator.

Reaganomics see **Reagan Ronald**

re-apportionment The re-drawing of constituency boundaries. Many political constituencies in the United States are defined on the basis of population. Each member of the US **House of Representatives**, for example, acts on behalf of approximately the same number of citizens. As a consequence, constituency boundaries have to be re-drawn periodically to accommodate demographic changes. Should a state's population rise at a faster rate, relative to other states, then it will be entitled to more representation in the House, and *vice versa*. Re-apportionment for the House occurs every ten years, following the results of the official US census. States, usually through a local legislative act, decide where any new constituency boundaries will be drawn. Re-apportionment is also referred to as 're-districting'.

recall election A poll held before the end of an official's term of office to determine whether this individual should continue in their post, or not. Approximately one-third of state constitutions contain provisions that, should citizens of that state be displeased, they may hold an election to remove a politician from office. Typically, a petition of signatures, numbering one-quarter of the total number of votes this politician originally polled, triggers a recall election. This official is then removed from office if 50 per cent of the votes cast call for this. A special election is subsequently held to fill the vacant post. Most famously, film actor Arnold Schwarzenegger was elected **Governor** of California in 2003, after the previous incumbent was removed from office by a recall election. No **federal government** posts are subject to recall.

reconstruction The collective name given to **federal government** programmes subsequent to the **civil war**, implemented between 1865 and 1877, setting the terms on which the rebellious southern states would be re-integrated back into the Union. Initially, these terms were quite moderate. However, after Confederate power structures began to resurface once more in southern state governments, along with **Jim Crow laws** undermining the rights of African-Americans, northern politicians sought to resist this return to the past. A period of 'radical reconstruction' ensued. Led by Republicans in the US **Congress**, legislation was passed to ensure martial law continued, that the Fifteenth Amendment to the US constitution was ratified, and that politicians loyal to the Union won office in the southern governments. Provision was also made to educate and feed ex-slaves. Eventually, however, civilian rule would return to the southern states, and with it the region's traditional political elite returned to office. These reinstated southern politicians revived legislation installing racial segregation once more. African-Americans would have to wait until the 1950s and 1960s, and the **civil rights movement,** for these Jim Crow laws to be removed permanently.

re-districting see **re-apportionment**

red state A state where the majority of the electorate support the Republican Party. Give that the United States has a **two-party system,** results of an election are often portrayed on a national map where the fifty states are either coloured blue (Democratic) or red (Republican) according to the party affiliation of the winning candidate.

Reform Party A political party born in 1995, in the wake of Ross **Perot**'s earlier presidential candidacy. Perot as the Reform Party candidate for **President** in 1996 won 8 per cent of the popular vote. When internal differences grew within the Reform Party during the 2000 election campaign, Perot cut his ties with this organisation, and it has subsequently splintered into a number of separate movements.

Website: http://www.reformparty.org

Regents of the University of California v. *Bakke,* **1978** see **affirmative action**

religious Right see **Christian Right**

reporting out When a Congressional committee agrees a final version of proposed legislation, and recommends this to the **floor** of the **Senate** or **House of Representatives.**

Republican National Committee The central, national, organisational body of the **Republican Party**. This committee helps co-ordinate the work of local, state and national Republican Party organisations and politicians, and promotes the election of its candidates via technical and financial support. In addition, the RNC oversees the quadrennial **national convention**, and the associated nomination of a Republican presidential candidate.

Website: http://www.rnc.org

Republican national convention see **national party convention**

Republican Party The Republican Party forms one half of the **two-party system** that has dominated US politics for over 150 years. Today, of the two major parties, the Republicans are the more libertarian, are socially conservative, favour less government intervention, have the closest links with business, and promote neo-liberal economic policies.

The Republican Party, or Grand Old Party (GOP) as it is also known, traces its roots back to opposition against the southern power block in the years prior to the **civil war**. Very much a northern party, support coalesced around northern industrial and financial interests against the sectional, states-rights agenda of the powerful **southern Democrats**. The nascent Republican Party was opposed to the spread of slavery: the issue that finally precipitated the civil war. The first Republican **President** was Abraham **Lincoln**.

The end of the civil war began a long period of Republican domination in US politics (the 1860s to the 1930s). The party's close identification with the Union victory in the war secured it the allegiance of most northern and midwestern farmers, while its support of protective tariffs and its accommodating attitude towards big business eventually gained this party the backing of powerful industrial and financial interests. This dominance, although interrupted occasionally in the early twentieth century, continued until the onset of the **Great Depression,** and the emergence of the **New Deal coalition.** The formation of this coalition would see the electoral pendulum swing back to the **Democratic Party** until the end of the 1960s.

The GOP has seen a gradual return to power in the last few decades. Aided by allegiances in the south switching from Democrat to Republican candidates (attracted by their socially conservative outlook), and the decline of the Democrat industrial-worker base, GOP presidents have occupied the **White House** for all but twelve years since 1969. Republican fortunes in the US **Congress** have also improved since the 1990s, with this party capturing both chambers for only the second time since 1931, after the 1995 elections. Today, with its neo-liberal economics and backing from the **Christian Right,** combined with an interventionist foreign policy (the 'War on Terror'), the GOP has moved a long way from its nineteenth-century roots, but is still the party of business.

Website: http://www.rnc.org

Republican revolution see **Contract with America**

reserved powers Reference to the powers that the US states kept for themselves when writing the US **constitution.** With this document, the states agreed to form the **federal government,** and, in so doing, gave up some of their powers. Certain specified political functions and duties were transferred from the states to the newly formed national government (these are known as the **delegated powers**). The states no longer took a lead, for instance, in foreign policy. Similarly, the states, via ratifying the **Bill of Rights,** also recognised that there are some areas where no government should legislate (the **denied powers**). These form the individual rights of US citizens. The constitution, for example, declares that no government may legislate away the freedom of speech. However, those powers that were not delegated to the federal government by the states, or retained by individual citizens, remain the **jurisdiction** of state governments: the so-called 'reserved powers'. Theoretically, therefore, sovereignty defaults to the states should it not match the aforementioned 'denied' or 'delegated' criteria. This dispensation is confirmed by the **Tenth Amendment** to the US constitution. In reality, however, the growth of the federal government, via the **necessary and proper clause** and **commerce clause,** has challenged this notion of state supremacy.

retail politics Political strategies and campaigns that are aimed at selling a candidate and policies to a broad, mass audience. Issues are generalised, and actions designed to generate mass appeal. The opposite of 'retail politics' is 'wholesale politics', where strategies are more focused, and tailored to appeal to a select group of more demanding customers/voters/interests.

revolutionary war Another name for the **War of Independence.** Most Americans refer to this event as the 'revolutionary war' or the 'American revolution'.

revolving door A term used to highlight the phenomenon where an individual may build a career working in institutions on both sides of a regulatory relationship. An official with the **Federal Election Commission,** for example, may start their career ensuring political parties abide by electoral law. The expertise this individual accumulates, however, is of use to the parties. As a consequence, they may be offered a job helping a party's relationship with the FEC: crossing to the other side of the divide. Later, the individual may move back to the FEC. Thus, personnel use a 'revolving door' that exists between institutions on either side of the regulatory line. They are 'gamekeepers turned poachers', or *vice versa*. Politicians who become journalists, sometimes later to return to public service, are also said to have gone through a 'revolving door'.

rider A clause added to a legislative bill.

right to bear arms see **Second Amendment**

RNC see **Republican National Committee**

Roe v. *Wade*, 1973 The **Supreme Court** decision that guarantees legal abortion in the United States. Abortion remains one of the most controversial and divisive social issues in this country.

In 1969, a woman from Texas (later known as Jane Roe, to protect her anonymity) sought an abortion. Her doctor refused on the grounds that Texas state law banned this procedure, unless a woman's life was in danger. Roe consequently sued the District Attorney for Dallas County (Henry Wade), claiming that her constitutional rights were being violated by the state of Texas. The Supreme Court agreed that Roe's **Fourteenth Amendment** and Ninth Amendment rights entitled her to a 'right of privacy', thus she should be able to make her own decision over whether to have an abortion or not. However, the opinion of the court also made it clear that this right to an abortion should be curtailed if there was a 'compelling state interest' to protect the health of the mother. States could thus still legislate to ban abortion in the third trimester (months seven to nine of a pregnancy). The Court expressed its opinion, however, that it would be unlikely that such compelling state interest would exist in the first trimester (months one to three). Since 1973, women in the United States have thus had the 'right to choose' when it comes to an abortion (should this entail no health danger to the mother).

With the Supreme Court growing more conservative in nature since the *Roe* v. *Wade* decision, abortion rights in the United States have been eroded. The case of *Webster* v. *Reproductive Health Services*, 1989, for example, places further restrictions on abortion justified by issues of maternal health, while *Rust* v. *Sullivan*, 1991 upheld government policy preventing clinics receiving **federal government** funds from performing abortions. Despite these cases, the central tenet of *Roe* v. *Wade*, a woman's 'right to choose', has yet to be overturned.

roll call Where the names of the members of the **House of Representatives** or **Senate** are called, to either establish whether the chamber is quorate, or to receive and record this individual's vote.

Roosevelt, Franklin D. (1882–1945) Of all the **Presidents** of the United States, Franklin Delano Roosevelt (FDR) has held this office for the longest period (1933 to 1945), and is the only individual to be elected to this post four times.

Roosevelt was raised in a wealthy New York state family and practised law before being elected to the New York state senate in 1910. He served as assistant secretary to the Navy in Woodrow **Wilson's** administration (1913–20), and then stood unsuccessfully as the

Democratic Party Vice President candidate in 1920. The following year, Roosevelt contracted polio and would be paralysed from the waist downwards for the rest of his life. He continued his career in New York politics, eventually becoming **Governor** of this state in 1929. Four years later he was elected to the **White House**.

FDR is remembered as the President that implemented the **New Deal** during the **Great Depression** of the 1930s, and as the President that led the United States into the Second World War, helping to defeat Nazi Germany. When Roosevelt arrived in Washington DC, the US economy was facing one of its worst crises ever: millions of Americans were unemployed, thousands of businesses were failing, and the banking and finance system was in chaos. Roosevelt's New Deal was a comprehensive set of measures, including banking reforms, economic regeneration initiatives, public works schemes, welfare reforms and labour legislation, aimed at tackling the economic turndown. Although historians still debate the extent to which FDR's policies helped the US economy recover, most agree that Roosevelt's leadership aided a restoration of public confidence, and contributed to the mitigation of the worst consequences of the depression.

Roosevelt, bowing to **isolationist** sentiment within the United States at the time, advocated US neutrality during the build-up to the Second World War. In 1939, however, this strict neutrality was broken when he recommended to **Congress** that the United States should be able to sell arms to those fighting the Axis powers. After Roosevelt broke tradition, and successfully stood for President a third time in 1940 (explained by the ominous international political situation), US neutrality was diluted even further when the US government 'loaned' Britain and its allies military equipment. Eventually, the United

States entered the war after the Japanese attack on Pearl Harbor late in 1941.

Today, most Americans look back kindly upon Franklin D. Roosevelt's career in the White House. He is seen as a great leader, first tackling the depression of the 1930s, and then directing the United States through the war years. FDR's most important *political* legacy, however, was building the **New Deal coalition**. This alignment of politicians, interest groups and voters, first brought together around the New Deal, continued to dominate national politics after FDR's death. This coalition ensured the Democratic Party's domination of the Congress for four decades (1930s, 1940s, 1950s and 1960s), providing a political base for the later administrations of John F. **Kennedy** and Lyndon B. **Johnson**.

rule of four see **certiorari, writ of**

rules committees Rules committees are the legislative forums where it is decided when (and if) a bill will be debated, for how long, and under what regulations. This procedural control make rules committees one of the most powerful in their respective chambers. For this reason, the most senior member of the majority party traditionally chairs the US House of Representatives Committee on Rules.

Unlike most of their equivalents, the **Senate** Committee on Rules and Administration is less powerful. This is because the Senate operates a principle of open debate. There are no official time limits set, and legislative procedure is generally determined by consensus between majority and minority party leaders. Consequently, the Senate committee deals more with administrative matters.

Websites: http://www.rules.house.gov and http://rules.senate.gov

running mate Parties nominate both a presidential and vice presidential candidate to stand in a **general election**. They campaign together as a team. The presidential nominee's choice of potential **Vice President** is known as his or her 'running mate'.

S

school district Local government in the United States is provided by a myriad of smaller administrative units authorised by state legislation. Existing alongside city and county councils are more specialised decision-making bodies. These 'special districts' tackle issues such as the provision of fire and rescue services, water management, environmental conservation, and even tasks such as the control of mosquitoes, in areas where this is a health problem. These special districts often have their own elected personnel, and many are funded by levies imposed on local communities (usually in the form of a property or sales tax). 'School districts' are another form of special district, administering educational establishments within a defined geographical area.

Scott v. *Sandford,* 1857 see *Dred Scott* v. *Sandford,* 1857

secession The act of withdrawing from a political union. In 1860–1, thirteen southern states withdrew from the United States to form their own **Confederate States of America,** precipitating the **civil war**. The Union government of **President** Abraham **Lincoln** declared this secession to be illegal, and forced these states back into the fold via military force. The **Supreme Court** in the case of *Texas* v. *White,* 1869 confirmed Lincoln's view that no state may secede from the Union.

Second Amendment The Second Amendment to the US **con-stitution, ratified** in 1791, is central to the controversial debate concerning gun ownership in the United States. The actual text of this amendment reads: 'A well-regulated Militia, being necessary to the security of a free State, the right of the people to keep and bear Arms, shall not be infringed.'

When the US constitution was ratified, each of the states had its own militia: a military force comprising ordinary citizens serving as part-time soldiers. Although the new constitution provided for a national standing army, it was thought that these militias should be maintained, to act as a **check and balance** on the federal force. The authors of the Second Amendment feared that this new federal army could become a tool of oppression. This was less likely to happen, however, if the 'people's' militias remained. Thus citizens should retain the right to own weapons.

In modern times, the Second Amendment has been referred to in a more general context. Pro-gun lobbies have tended to concentrate on just one clause of the sentence that comprises the Second Amendment: 'the right of the people to keep and bear Arms'. Organisations, such as the **National Rifle Association**, use this clause to promote the freedom of gun ownership in the United States. The majority of public opinion tends to support this view. Governments, as a consequence, have only enacted limited gun control legislation, the banning of sophisticated assault weapons, for example, and, in some states, carrying a concealed weapon.

As yet, no part of the judiciary in the United States has directly defined to what extent US citizens do have a right of gun ownership under the Second Amendment. The **Supreme Court**, in particular, has not cared to interpret the constitution with respect to the relationship between this right and being a member of a 'well-regulated militia', despite having the opportunity to do so on several occasions. The Court has chosen not to issue writs of *certiorari* in these cases.

Secretary of State The individual within the **executive branch** of the **federal government** who takes responsibility for implementing US foreign policy. This person is head of the **Department of State,** is a **cabinet** member, and a leading advisor to the **President.** Additionally, the holder of this office is the first cabinet member in the line of **presidential succession.** Should the posts of President, **Vice President, Speaker of the House,** and **president pro tempore of the Senate** be vacant simultaneously, the Secretary of State will become Acting President.

Website: http://www.state.gov/secretary

segregation see **Jim Crow laws**

Senate The upper chamber of the US **Congress.** The Senate comprises one hundred elected members, with two senators representing each state. Each of these members' term of office lasts six years, with one-third of the chamber being elected every two years. The presiding officer of the Senate is the US **Vice President,** who may only vote to break a tie. Apart from such votes, and occasional ceremonial duties, much of the Vice President's work in this body is carried out by a deputy, the **president pro tempore of the Senate.**

The Senate's primary function, together with the **House of Representatives,** is to make federal law. Each chamber acts as a **check and balance** on the other. The House and Senate differ in their constituencies (the House represents districts determined by population), their impeachment role (the House charges, while the Senate tries), and in the fact that the Senate has the sole power of 'advise and consent' (confirming the **President**'s appointments, and ratifying treaties). Enjoying longer terms of office than members of the House, and representing states rather than smaller constituencies, the Senate often positions itself further from the more confrontational day-to-day politics of the lower chamber. Instead, the Senate takes a more deliberative approach to its legislative duties. There are no time restrictions, for example, on a member's right to debate an issue. The Senate convenes in the **Capitol Building** in **Washington DC.**

Website: http://www.senate.gov/

Senate Committee on Appropriations The Senate Appropriations Committee is the largest committee of this chamber. Its role is defined by the US **constitution**, which requires 'appropriations made by law' prior to the expenditure of any money from the federal treasury. The Committee writes the legislation that allocates federal funds to the numerous agencies, departments and organisations of the **executive branch** on an annual basis. Given that the content of this legislation determines whether federal programmes are fully or partially funded, or not at all, this is one of the most powerful committees, together with its House equivalent, found in **Congress.**

Website: http://appropriations.senate.gov

Senate Committee on Rules and Administration see **rules committees**

Senate, president pro tempore see **president pro tempore of the Senate**

seniority Reference to the privileges, and the more powerful appointments, that length of continuous service brings within the US **Congress**. Those who have served the longest within the US **Senate** or **House of Representatives** will be appointed to the more powerful positions and committees of these chambers (leadership roles, for example, or chairs of appropriations, ways and means, or rules committees). Senior members will also receive other benefits, such as being allocated the largest offices on **Capitol Hill**.

The stranglehold of seniority over the **committee system** reached its zenith in the 1940s, 1950s and 1960s. The success of the **New Deal coalition** resulted in a block of **southern Democrats** gaining seniority within Congress. Occupying safe constituencies, being returned election after election, these individuals used their seniority to dominate both House and Senate institutions for decades. Collectively they occupied committee chairs and were appointed to leadership roles. Many argue that having legislative leaders from one party and one geographical area, associated with certain social views, for so long, distorted the representative role of Congress.

The seniority stranglehold was lessened in 1953 with the **Johnson Rule**, which stated that no **Democratic Party** senator should be awarded a second major committee chair until all had received a first appointment. It was not until the 1970s, however, that the **sub-committee Bill of Rights** was pushed though by liberal (as opposed to southern) Democrats. These reforms increased the independence of sub-committees, lessening the ability of their parent committee chairs to make appointments and set agendas. Similarly, seniority was made only one of several criteria used to determine the allocations of positions to party members within Congress. Seniority, however, is still an issue in the House and Senate today. As late as 1995, Republicans decided that no member could chair a committee or sub-committee for more than six years.

separate but equal see *Plessy v. Ferguson*, 1896

separation of the powers Article One, Section Three of the US **constitution** states, 'The powers of government shall be divided into three distinct departments: legislative, executive and judicial. No person or persons belonging to or constituting one of these departments shall exercise any of the powers properly belonging to either of the others . . .' This separation of powers is designed so no one institution or individual within the system of government becomes too powerful. Power is fragmented. Consequently, government can only function when its different divisions cooperate.

September the Eleventh see **9/11**

shared powers see **concurrent powers**

Sierra Club An interest group campaigning on environmental issues.
   Website: http://www.sierraclub.org

Smoke-filled rooms An expression used to signify political decision-making conducted in secret, where an elite group will decide amongst themselves a desired outcome. This expression was first used in 1920, when the **Republican Party** was in deadlock at its **national convention** over whom to **nominate** as their presidential candidate. A powerful group of party senators retired to a 'smoke-filled room', away from the convention **floor**, to intrigue late into the night, and eventually agreed amongst themselves to back the nomination of Warren G.

Harding. The convention floor confirmed this decision the next day.

soft money If **hard money** stems from political donations spent directly on an individual's electoral campaign, soft money is the term used to describe contributions used more broadly by political parties. As a consequence, soft money is free of many legal restrictions imposed by **campaign finance reform**. Examples of soft money spending include drives to increase voter registration, the capacity-building of political parties at local level, and voter education on a myriad of issues. Controversy surrounds soft money, however, as donations are often used to support party officers and personnel utilised, but not paid for, by candidates running for election, or to buy television **issue advertisements** that, although they do not specifically endorse a candidate, infer this, or attempt to discredit an opponent's campaign.

Solicitor General An officer appointed by the **President** of the United States to represent the **executive branch** in the **Supreme Court**. The Solicitor General is a deputy of the **Attorney General** in the Department of Justice.
    Website: http://www.usdoj.gov/osg

solid south see **southern Democrats**

southern Democrats A block of **Democratic Party** supporters residing in the southern region of the United States. The Democratic Party was established as a movement of agrarian interests, which opposed the centralisation of government. These sentiments made this party popular in the south amongst the planter elite and those distrustful of the industrial power growing in the north of the country. The southern states became solidly Democratic as a result. This remained the case, despite the northern and southern wings of the party disagreeing over slavery at the time of the **civil war**. Indeed, it was southern Democrats who provided the political leadership that brought **secession**, and the formation of the **Confederate States of America**.

After the civil war, the Democratic Party continued to benefit from the 'solid south'. A deep resentment of the **Republican Party**, the party that had prosecuted the war against the Confederacy, ensured that Democrats were returned in state and federal elections in this region time after time. Southern Democrats now advocated states' rights, under which justification they perpetuated a system of segregation and discrimination in this region of the United States. Given that southern Democrats enjoyed **incumbency** in the 'solid south', they gained **seniority** in the US **Congress**, and legislators from this political block dominated this intuition from the 1930s through to the 1960s.

The Democratic Party's domination of the south began to fade in the 1960s, when many supporters became disillusioned with the party's liberal leadership. Southern Democrats, being conservative in outlook, disapproved of the party supporting the **civil rights movement**, and its willingness to sanction government intervention to provide welfare support. Given their social conservatism and their preference for states' rights over federal intervention (and unrepentant racism, in some cases), many southern Democrats re-aligned themselves, and began to vote for the Republican Party. Instead of being a Democratic 'solid south', this region is today now more likely to elect Republican representatives. This tension between conservatism and the modern Democratic Party is demonstrated in the willingness of remaining southern Democrats to frequently cross party lines: see **boll weevils, Blue Dog Democrats,** and **Reagan Democrats.**

Speaker of the House of Representatives The presiding officer of the US **House of Representatives,** and usually the leader of the majority party in this chamber. The Speaker is appointed through a vote of House members. This individual is second in the presidential line of succession, and will become Acting President if the presidency and the Vice presidency are vacant concurrently.

Website: http://speaker.house.gov

special districts Local government in the United States is provided by a myriad of smaller administrative units authorised by state legislation. Existing alongside city and county councils are more specialised decision-making bodies. These 'special districts' tackle issues such as the provision of fire and rescue services, water management, environmental conservation, school administration, and even tasks such as the control of mosquitoes, in areas where this is a health problem. These special districts often have their own elected personnel, and many are funded by levies imposed on local communities (usually in the form of property or sales taxes).

Spirit of the Laws see **Montesquieu, Baron de**

split-ticket voting Where a member of the electorate votes for candidates of more than one political party on the same ballot paper. On the same polling day, for example, an individual may vote for a Republican **President,** while at the same time voting for a Democratic senatorial candidate. Split-ticket voting is more common in the United States than in other democracies due to weaker party allegiances.

spoils system The practice of rewarding loyal party supporters with appointments to public office, when this party forms a government. In more modern times, although parties still operate a spoils system, it is expected that nominees for public office possess competency and expertise in the post for which they have been selected.

State Department see **Department of State**

state of emergency Where a political administration declares that certain functions of government and/or laws have been suspended. This may be in response to events such as natural disasters, or military or civil unrest. States of emergency are rare in most democracies, but more common in the United States. This is due to the fact that a declaration of an emergency by a **governor** or mayor permits the **federal government** to commit national resources to the problem. States of emergency are therefore commonly called after a severe flood, hurricane or forest fire.

State of the Union Address The title of the speech given by the US **President** to **Congress**, more recently at the start of each year, outlining the **chief executive's** opinion on how the US government is faring, and explaining proposed initiatives.

states' rights The protection and promotion of state government policies over those of the **federal government**. Most obviously, issues of states' rights became prominent in US history throughout the period leading up to the **civil war** (where the southern states wished to retain the institution of slavery), and during the **civil rights** campaign of the 1950s and 1960s (where the southern states wished to retain policies of segregation). The twentieth century saw a significant expansion of the role of the federal government, sometimes at the expense of states' rights. Legally, this expansion is supported by the **Supreme Court** ruling of *McCulloch* v. *Maryland,* **1819,** which declared that the federal government commands not only **enumerated powers** under the US **constitution,** but also **implied powers.**

strict construction A narrow interpretation of a legal document. A judge or politician who subjects the US **constitution** to strict construction, for example, will try to ascertain precisely what the **Founding Fathers** intended. No allowances are made for the fact that this document was penned in the nineteenth century, and that modern-day society has developed a different set of principles and values. The literal meanings of the words are adhered to. Strict constructionalists are also known as 'intentionalists' and 'originalists'. The opposite of a strict constructionist is one who applies **flexible construction.**

stump speech A term used in reference to a politician's stock address, used several times during a campaign, at different venues, perhaps with only minor variations.

Sub-committee A method of dividing up the work of a committee. The US Senate Committee on Foreign Relations, for example, currently has seven sub-committees: 'African Affairs', 'East Asian and Pacific Affairs', 'European Affairs', 'International Economic Policy, Export and Trade Promotion', 'International Operations and Terrorism', 'Near Eastern and South Asian Affairs', 'Western Hemisphere, Peace Corp and Narcotics Affairs'. All sub-committees refer their work to their parent, full committee, before legislation is **reported** to the **floor** of the **Senate** or **House of Representatives.**

sub-committee Bill of Rights Reforms made during the early 1970s modifying the **committee system** of the US **Congress**. The 'sub-committee Bill of Rights' authorised **House of Representatives** sub-committees to meet under their own authority and hold hearings, as well as acting upon matters referred to them. This broke the stranglehold of the parent committee chairs, who previously had controlled the business of the sub-committees. Now sub-committees could act independently. This challenged the **seniority** system prevalent in Congress at the time.

subpoena A writ ordering a person to attend a legal hearing, or to provide evidence to this body. The right of the US **Congress** to subpoena witnesses and evidence is written into the US **constitution**. Refusal to testify before this body, having been subpoenaed, may result in a prison sentence for 'contempt of Congress'. Most famously, **President** Richard **Nixon**, claiming **executive privilege**, refused a Congressional subpoena during the **Watergate** investigations. The President lost the subsequent **Supreme Court** case, *United States* v. *Nixon,* **1974,** and subsequently resigned.

sunshine rules Reference to reforms of the **committee system** in the US **Congress**, resulting in nearly all committee meetings being open to the public. Sunshine rules were adopted by the **House of Representatives** in 1973 and the **Senate** in 1975. Previously, the administrative and mark-up business of these committees was conducted behind closed doors.

Super Tuesday A date in early March of a presidential election year where several states, since 1988, have simultaneously held **primary elections**. Given the number of national convention delegates elected on Super Tuesday, a candidate failing to secure significant support at these polls is unlikely to win his or her party's nomination.

super delegates Individuals who are invited to attend a national party convention, rather than qualifying to do so via primary elections. These super delegates have the same voting rights as the elected delegates, giving them an equal say in who will be the party's presidential nominee and what the party's platform will consist of. Super delegates are largely drawn from the ranks of a party's leadership (members of Congress and the national committees, for example) and from employees of relevant interest groups.

Supremacy Clause The sentence in Article Six of the US constitution that articulates that the constitution itself, federal laws, and treaties signed by the United States override state laws.

Supreme Court As its name suggests, the Supreme Court is the highest judicial body to be found in the United States. It acts as the final court of appeal, and has the final say over interpreting the US constitution. The Court currently comprises nine justices, although Congress has varied this number over time, and it is led by a Chief Justice. Suitable candidates are nominated by the President to serve the Court when a position becomes vacant on the death, impeachment or retirement of a sitting judge. The President's choice is then confirmed (or not) by the US Senate. Once appointed, no justice may be removed from power unless they are impeached. This security of tenure is designed to prevent political pressure being placed on Court members.

Much of the Supreme Court's political influence stems from its power of **judicial review**. This power is not specifically outlined in the US constitution, but the Court took this role upon itself with the **opinion** of *Marbury* v. *Madison,* 1803. From this date, the Supreme Court has had the ability to strike down acts of Congress, or acts from state legislatures, as well as executive policies, should they be deemed to be in conflict with the constitution. Women in the United States, for example, gained the right to choose whether to have an abortion, or not, when the Court found Texas law on this issue to violate the constitutional rights of citizens (*Roe* v. *Wade,* 1973). Similarly, earlier, the Court hastened the end of **segregation** in the southern states with its opinion of *Brown* v. *Board of Education,* 1954, which found the state of Kansas to be denying African-American school children their constitutional rights. What the court may not do, however, is directly intervene in an issue, of its own accord. A citizen must first bring a case in a lower court, which is subsequently appealed through the system to the Supreme Court. The Supreme Court is at liberty to choose cases from any of the numerous appeals it receives. Successful applications receive a writ of **certiorari**.

Website: http://www.supremecourtus.gov

swing state A state where no political party dominates, and consequently elections are competitive. New Jersey, for example, has been a 'swing state' in recent elections, switching several times between providing respective victories for the **Demoractic Party** and the **Republican Party**. As the outcome of elections in swing states is uncertain, parties focus campaign resources in these areas, as this is where national elections are won and lost.

T

Tammany Hall Literally, the host building of the head-quarters of the **Democratic Party** in New York City. Tammany Hall, however, has become a by-word in US politics describing a well-organised, urban, political machine. The phrase is often used in a pejorative sense, as Democrats in New York City often gave out favours in return for votes. The success of the Tammany Hall system can be judged by the fact that the Democratic Party dominated this city's government from the 1850s to the 1930s, and this machine still had significant influence as late as the 1960s.

Teamsters union The International Brotherhood of Teamsters, Chauffeurs, Warehousemen, Stablemen and Helpers of America was formed in 1903, after the merger of two labour organisations representing delivery men (using horse-drawn vehicles). It grew to be the largest trade union in the Unites States by 1940, enlarged further after organising and recruiting amongst truck drivers. A strongly centralised union, the Teamsters were able to negotiate nationwide freight haulage agreements on behalf of their members. The reputation of the union was tarnished, however, by its leadership's association with racketeering, organised crime and the manipulation of the union's pension fund. Between 1957 and 1988 three of the Teamsters' presidents were convicted of criminal charges and sentenced to prison terms. These activities led to this union being expelled from the **American Federation of Labor and Congress of Industrial Organizations** in 1957, and only being readmitted thirty years later.

Website: http://www.teamster.org

Tenth Amendment The Tenth Amendment to the US **constitution,** ratified in 1791, as part of the **Bill of Rights,** states: 'The powers not delegated to the United States by the Constitution, nor prohibited by it to the States, are reserved to the States respectively, or to the people.' This part of the constitution reinforces the fact that the **federal government** was established to carry out specific functions on behalf of the United States: the so-called **delegated powers**. Additionally, no government was able to legislate in certain areas of society, due to the individual rights of US citizens (the **denied powers**). What the Tenth Amendment clarifies, however, is that power not denied to all governments, or specifically delegated to the federal government, remains within the **jurisdiction** of the state governments (the **reserved powers**). It is a catch-all clause, added by the states to preserve their sovereignty within the United States. The Tenth Amendment, to an extent, conflicts with the **necessary and proper** clause and the **commerce clause**. These two sentences of the constitution have allowed federal government to expand at the states' expense for more than 200 years.

term limit The legal prevention of an individual standing for an elected post, once this person has served a stipulated number of terms in that same office. The Twenty-second Amendment to the US **constitution,** ratified in 1951, for example, decrees that no politician may be elected **President** of the United States more than twice. In other words, under normal circumstances (see **Twenty-second Amendment**), Presidents are restricted to holding this office for a maximum of two four-year terms. Supporters of term limits argue that these restrictions aid the renewal of government, bringing new personnel and ideas to the institutions of power, helping the democratic process.

Texas v. *White*, 1869 see **secession**

Thirteenth Amendment An 1865 **constitutional amendment**, ratified in the wake of the **civil war**, which abolished slavery in the United States.

ticket A phrase used in elections where more than one office is determined by a voter's choice. A presidential candidate and a vice presidential candidate, for example, are said to be 'running on the same ticket'. 'Ticket' is also used to indicate a candidate's party: 'Jones is running on a Republican ticket.'

Tocqueville, Alexis de (1805–59) A nineteenth-century French political philosopher and historian whose observations of US politics during the 1830s were published in his book: *Democracy in America*. This work has become a standard text discussing conditions favouring and threatening democracy.

  Suggested reading: Alexis de Tocqueville, *Democracy in America* (New York: Harper, 1988).

Tonkin Resolution see **Gulf of Tonkin**

traditional presidency Where the **President** of the United States acts more in the role envisaged by the **Founding Fathers**, implementing policy, rather than initiating it. Agenda-setting is left more to the **Congress**. Many see the 'traditional president' being eclipsed by the **modern president** with the arrival of Franklin D. **Roosevelt** in the **White House**, with his **New Deal**.

Treasury see **Department of the Treasury**

Truman Doctrine A pledge made by **President** Harry S. **Truman,** in an address before the US **Congress** in 1947, that stated the United States would assist governments resisting communism throughout the world. This doctrine subsequently became a key strategy in the prosecution of the Cold War.

Truman, Harry S. (1884–1972) The thirty-third **President** of the United States, holding office between 1945 and 1953. Raised on a Missouri farm, Truman gained employment in a myriad of (none too successful) jobs and business partnerships before serving in the US Army during World War One. On returning to the United States, and another failed business partnership, he entered state politics. Association with the boss of a local **Democratic Party** machine in Missouri saw Truman first serve as a county judge (1922 to 1934), and then enter the US **Senate**. Truman managed to rise above the criminal convictions of his former associates in the Missouri Democratic Party and win re-election to the Senate in 1940. In 1944, Truman received his party's **nomination** as candidate for **Vice President,** and secured victory alongside Franklin D. **Roosevelt** in the **general election** of that year. His term as US Vice President lasted just eighty-two days, where upon Truman became President as a result of Roosevelt's death in office. Truman won a presidential election in his own right in 1948.

Truman's presidency was dominated by foreign affairs: the end of World War Two, and the subsequent development of the Cold War. Soon after becoming President, Truman took the decision to use atomic weapons against Japan, to terminate hostilities quickly. Yet, having helped defeat fascism, the United States immediately had to deal with communist expansion. Truman supported a confrontational policy of 'containment' against the Soviet Union and Communist China. Liberal democracies were supported financially in

Europe (the Marshall Plan), NATO was formed, and US troops saw active duty, in the name of containment, in Korea.

In terms of domestic policy, Truman had some successes in building upon the provisions of the **New Deal**, but he also had to spend time resisting **Republican Party** efforts to repeal some of Roosevelt's earlier reforms. Truman's unpopularity as a result of post-war inflation, labour unrest, and US involvement in the Korean War persuaded the President not to seek re-election in 1953, at the end of his first full term in office.

Twelfth Amendment An amendment to the US **constitution**, ratified in 1804, that altered the manner in which US **Vice Presidents** are elected. Previously, members of the **electoral college** each had two votes on the same ballot. The winner of this poll would become **President**, while the runner-up would be Vice President. The Twelfth Amendment separates the election of President and Vice President. The electoral college now conducts two separate polls. This ensured that the President and Vice President, from this date onwards, came from the same political party.

Twenty-fifth Amendment An amendment to the US **constitution**, ratified in 1967, addressing two issues of **succession** within the **executive branch** of the **federal government**. In the first instance, this amendment outlines procedure should the **President** become incapacitated, and, second, it determines the rules for appointing a new **Vice President**, should this position become vacant.

In terms of outlining procedure should the President become disabled, the Vice President becomes Acting President if invited to do so by the President. Should there be no such invitation, the Vice President may declare the

President unfit for office, and become Acting President him or herself, but only if supported by a majority of the **cabinet**. In either scenario, it is the President him or herself who determines when they are able to return to office. If the Acting President and a majority of the cabinet disagree with the President's decision to return to office, the matter is referred to the US **Senate**. A two-thirds majority vote is required to maintain an Acting President in office against the wishes of the President.

The Twenty-fifth amendment also makes provision for appointing a Vice President, should this position become vacant between general elections. Previously, the post was left unfilled should an incumbent resign, be impeached or die in office. Since 1967, however, with the ratification of this amendment, the President may now nominate a replacement. This nomination must be confirmed by a majority vote in both chambers of **Congress**.

This amendment, with respect to replacing the Vice President, became almost immediately relevant when Richard **Nixon**'s Vice President, Spiro **Agnew**, resigned in 1973. Nixon appointed **Speaker of the House, Gerald Ford**, as his new Vice President. Ford then succeeded Nixon to the presidency itself upon Nixon's own resignation over the **Watergate** affair. Ford had thus become President without being elected to this post or to the Vice presidency.

Twenty-second Amendment An amendment to the US **constitution**, ratified in 1951, setting a **term limit** on the office of the **President**. Under normal circumstances, no President of the United States may serve more than two four-year periods in office. This limit is designed as a **check and balance** to prevent any one individual dominating the **executive branch** for too long a period. The first US President, George **Washington**, who retired from this post after eight years' service, set the precedent of a two-term spell. Three Presidents have sought a third term, but only Franklin D. **Roosevelt** was elected to do this (and was, indeed, returned for a fourth term). Debate about the need for presidential term limits commenced soon after Roosevelt died in office.

Theoretically, an individual could serve as President for just less than ten years. Such an individual would have been promoted to the presidency due to the death, resignation or impeachment of an incumbent, and then be elected to this post twice after the original succession (two four-year elected terms, plus less than two years as a 'replacement' President). The Twenty-second Amendment states that anyone becoming President in these circumstances, and serving more than two years as a 'stand-in' President, may only seek election to this post once.

Twin Towers Reference to the World Trade Center building in New York City, targeted in the **9/11** terrorist attacks.

two-party system Reference to the fact that, since the organisation of political parties in the United States, no more than two parties have dominated the competition for government in this country. Subsequent to the **civil war**, this contest for power has been between the **Republican Party** and the **Democratic Party**. Third parties have difficulty competing with established contenders due to the nature of majoritarian electoral systems of the United States. However, successful third-party campaigns have occasionally prompted policy changes or a realignment within the two dominant parties. Ross **Perot**, for example, ran a successful third-party campaign in 1992 (polling 19 per cent of the popular vote in the presidential race), but his **Reform Party** won no seats in **Congress**. Responding to this challenge, the Republican and Democratic parties altered their subsequent polices as a result. They both added Perot's main demand to their own party platform: balanced budgets to address the **national debt**.

U

Uncle Tom A pejorative term for an African-American who defers too easily to white authority. The phrase is derived from Harriet Beecher Stowe's novel *Uncle Tom's Cabin*, where the title character, a slave, is a long-suffering, faithful servant of his white owners.

Further reading: Harriet Beecher Stowe, *Uncle Tom's Cabin* (London: Prentice Hall, 2003)

underground railway see **abolitionists**

United States Conference of Mayors A non-partisan organisation bringing together some 1,100 mayoral offices nationwide. The Conference offers opportunities for networking, assists federal–city relationships, and provides leadership on issues relating to urban and suburban policy.

Website: http://www.usmayors.org

United States v. *Darby Lumber Company*, **1941** see **commerce clause**

United States v. *Nixon*, **1974** A **Supreme Court** decision outlining the extent of **executive privilege**. As part of its investigation into the **Watergate** affair, the US **Senate** requested copies of recordings made of **Oval Office** conversations between the **President** and his staff. President Richard **Nixon** refused this **subpoena** on the grounds of **executive privilege**. The Court ruled that although the US **constitution** supported the notion of executive privilege (particularly in cases of national security), the right to a fair trial outweighed these considerations. No official should be immune from the judicial process on the grounds of executive privilege, or the **separation of the powers**. Nixon complied with the Court's **opinion**, and released the tapes to **Congress**. He resigned as President shortly afterwards.

University of California v. *Bakke*, **1978** see **affirmative action**

V

veto The right to reject a legislative act, making it null and void. As part of a system of **checks and balances** in the United States, the US **President** has the right to veto Congressional proposals, while **governors** may reject bills from state legislators. In the case of the **federal government**, Congress may override a presidential veto by a two-thirds majority vote in both the **House of Representatives** and the **Senate**.

   See also: **pocket veto** and **line-item veto**

veto override see **veto**

veto, pocket see **pocket veto**

Vice President The US Vice President (VP) has two constitutional functions within the US system of government: he or she succeeds the **President** should the incumbent resign, be incapacitated, impeached or die in office; he or she also has a ceremonial function within the US **Senate**, and has a casting say in this chamber, should there be a tied vote.

   Beyond these constitutional duties, Vice Presidents have, in more modern times, become key policy advisors to the President. Although the President has no official authority over the Vice President, and may not dismiss him or her, VPs often accept this advisory role to advance their own political career: perhaps grooming themselves for the presidency itself.

To become US Vice President, politicians first have to be selected by a party's presidential nominee, to act as their **running mate**. The choice of running mate usually reflects an attempt to balance the party's presidential **ticket**. A vice presidential candidate from a different region than that of the presidential candidate, or one representing a different wing of the party, makes the party's ticket more attractive. This choice is confirmed by a vote of the **national party convention**. The presidential and vice presidential nominees then campaign together to try and win the **White House** in the November **general election**.

Website: http://www.whitehouse.gov/vicepresident

Vietnam War US involvement in Vietnam dated from the administration of Harry S. **Truman**, when economic and military aid was provided to deter a communist takeover of French Indochina. When France withdrew from this country in 1954, and Vietnam was divided into two separate states, the US continued to support anti-communist forces in the south. A decade later, communist insurgents threatened to overwhelm the government of South Vietnam. In 1964, following an allegedly unprovoked attack on US warships patrolling the **Gulf of Tonkin**, a resolution pledging support for American action in Vietnam was passed by the US **Congress**. This Tonkin Resolution was used by the administration of Lyndon B. **Johnson** to justify a massive commitment of US troops to this war. Military operations spread to North Vietnam, Cambodia and Laos. Amid heavy US and Vietnamese casualties, and the failure to defeat the communist insurgents, a vocal anti-war movement grew in the United States. Effective defeat in Vietnam has scarred US society for several generations. The Nixon Administration eventually withdrew American troops from south-east Asia in 1973. Lacking US military support, the southern government finally fell to the North Vietnamese army in 1975, whereupon the country was reunited under communist rule.

Voting Rights Act, 1965 An act of **Congress** that specifically outlawed practices such as grandfather clauses, literacy tests and poll taxes that had been used in the southern states, up to this point, to disenfranchise African-Americans. The federal government's Department of Justice was empowered to scrutinise state electoral laws. The number of African-Americans who voted after the passage of this act increased dramatically. For example, in 1960, only 5 per cent of those African-Americans eligible to vote in the state of Mississippi did so. By 1968, this figure had risen to 60 per cent.

W

War of 1812 see **Madison, James**

War on Poverty Another slogan for **President** Lyndon B. Johnson's 1960s **Great Society reforms.**

War Powers Resolution, 1973 Legislation that requires the **President** to receive the consent of the US **Congress** when deploying military forces in combat situations. The US **constitution** states that only Congress has the right to declare war, after which the President, as **Commander in Chief,** prosecutes military action. Yet the United States has only officially declared war five times (the **War of 1812**, the Mexican–American War, the Spanish–American War, World War I and World War II). Other military campaigns, successive Presidents have argued, particularly in recent decades, have been actions short of war: merely police actions. They have not required a formal Congressional declaration of war.

Congress in the early 1970s became hostile to President Richard **Nixon**'s military operations in south-east Asia, in particular his secret bombing of Cambodia. The **legislative branch** therefore passed the War Powers Resolution to provide a **check and balance** on 'police actions'. The Resolution requires the President, should he or she deploy combat troops, to inform Congress of this action within forty-eight hours of the event. The President must then receive Congressional approval of this military campaign within sixty days of the first deployment. This may be in the form of a formal declaration of war, or legislation endorsing the action. Congress may grant an extension to this sixty-day period. If no such consent is forthcoming, the President must withdraw US troops from the relevant theatre of war within a further sixty days.

The War Powers Resolution was passed by the US Congress, overriding the **veto** of Richard Nixon. Several subsequent Presidents have declared the Resolution to be unconstitutional. Most have largely ignored the legislation when deploying US troops. The constitutional validity of the Resolution remains uncertain. When called upon to express an opinion on the matter with the case of *Crockett* v. *Reagan*, 1982, the **judicial branch** ducked the responsibility, ruling that it was an issue for the executive and legislative branches to sort out themselves; not a matter for the courts.

Warren Court see **Warren, Earl**

Warren, Earl (1891–1974) Served as **governor** of California between 1943 and 1953, before being appointed by **President** Dwight **Eisenhower** to be **Chief Justice** of the **Supreme Court**. Warren remained in this post until his death in 1974. Warren's record, serving as a district attorney in several counties, **Attorney General**, and then a **Republican Party** Governor of California, suggested that he was a conservative. It was this record in public office that attracted the attention of Eisenhower. Yet Eisenhower called his decision to appoint Warren to the Supreme Court, 'the biggest dam-fool mistake I ever made.' This is because Warren presided over one of the most radical Supreme Courts the United States has ever seen. His Court advanced individual freedoms (particularly for those accused of crimes) and increased the people's representation in government. The Warren Court, for example, authored the **opinions** of *Brown* v. *Board of Education*, 1954; *Gideon* v. *Wainwright*, 1963; and *Miranda* v. *Arizona*, 1966. Warren believed the Supreme Court should protect the rights of individuals against the state, and that **judicial activism** could help the other branches of government meet their responsibilities.

Washington Beltway The name of the ring-road circling **Washington DC**. Political insiders, privy to the workings of the **federal government** within the capital city, are often described as being 'inside the Beltway'.

Washington DC The capital city of the United States of America, and host to the leading institutions of the US **federal government**. Given that this city is home to all three branches of the national government, housing the **White House**, the **Congress** and the **Supreme Court**, the phrase 'Washington DC' is often used simply as a synonym for the federal government itself. Washington city is located in the federal territory of the **District of Columbia**.

Washington, George (1732–99) First **President** of the United States, holding office between 1789 and 1797. Washington is the country's original national hero, having lead American forces to victory against the British in the **War of Independence**, and then helping secure a civilian, representative government in its aftermath (despite support for him to lead a more authoritarian regime). Washington retired from the presidency after two terms of office, setting a precedent of **term limits**.

Washington's farewell address An open letter to the American people, published by George **Washington** in the form of a speech, in 1796, on the occasion of his retirement from the presidency. An original draft of this address was penned by James **Madison** four years earlier, when it appeared Washington might retire after just one term in office. This draft was revised by Alexander **Hamilton**, with Washington finalising his valedictory advice. Domestically, the address urged Americans not to enter into sectional politics, and especially not to form competing political parties. In foreign affairs, Washington warned about the dangers of permanent 'entangling' alliances, advocating instead a more **isolationist** stance.

Watergate A political scandal of the early 1970s that forced Richard **Nixon** to resign: the first US **President** ever to do this. In June 1972, five individuals broke into **Washington DC**'s Watergate office complex. The particular office suite targeted was that occupied by the **Democratic National Committee**. Two years of investigations by the police, the District Attorney, journalists from the *Washington Post*, the Department of Justice, and **Congress** identified personnel from Nixon's Committee to Re-Elect the President to be complicit in this break-in. This was part of a wider conspiracy to disrupt and harass Nixon's political opponents: operation Gemstone.

Initially, the **White House** denied any 'involvement whatsoever' in this 'third-rate burglary'. However, members of the Nixon Administration did attempt to cover up the existence of operation Gemstone. The **Central Intelligence Agency** (CIA), for example, was instructed to impede the enquiry of the **Federal Bureau of Investigation** (FBI). Eventually, investigators linked Nixon to the subsequent cover-up measures, if not the original burglary itself. The key piece of evidence was contained within recorded **Oval Office** conversations. These tapes were only released by the President to **Senate** investigators after the **Supreme Court** decision of *United States* v. *Nixon*, 1973. The House Committee on the Judiciary voted to **impeach** Nixon on charges of obstructing justice. He resigned before the Senate had the opportunity to try him. The legacy of the Watergate scandal has been less trust in the Office of the President ever since, and the growth of media scrutiny of government, in the form of investigative journalism.

Ways and Means Committee see **House of Representatives Ways and Means Committee**

West Wing Part of the **White House** building housing the **Oval Office** and working accommodation for senior staff of the **executive branch**.

Whig Party A political party in US history, most powerful in the 1840s and 1850s. The Whigs formed during the 1930s in opposition to Andrew **Jackson's Democratic Party**. They rejected Jackson's leadership style of a strong

executive branch, and favoured industrial development over Democratic agrarian interests. The party disintegrated in the second half of the 1850s over the issue of slavery, making way for the **Republican Party** as the Democrat's main opponent in the **two-party system**.

whip Deputies of the majority and minority leaders in legislative bodies charged with organising support for a party's bill. Whips identify who will back a proposal, and then make sure that votes are cast. These posts are modelled on the British parliamentary system. The word 'whip' is derived from the 'whipper-in' of a hunt, who insures that hounds do not stray too far during the chase.

White House The building, located at 1600 Pennsylvania Avenue, **Washington DC,** that is the official residence of the **President** of the United States. This building has formerly been known as the 'President's Palace', the 'President's House', and the 'Executive Mansion', before officially becoming the 'White House' in 1901, during the presidency of Theodore **Roosevelt**. Contained within the White House are rooms that make up the living accommodation of the President and his or her family, a ballroom and dining room for official functions, a vast collection of offices for the President's staff, a communications centre, and catering and medical facilities for all the building's inhabitants.

Whitewater A financial scandal of the 1990s revolving around the Whitewater Development Company, of which **First Lady** Hillary Rodham Clinton and **President** Bill **Clinton** were directors. Although the Clintons were cleared of any wrongdoing with respect to this incident, the report of the Independent Counsel of the Department of Justice, Kenneth Starr, who investigated these accusations, brought to light the President's sexual improprieties with Monica **Lewinsky**. This later resulted in an unsuccessful effort to **impeach** Clinton.

wholesale politics Political strategies and campaigns where actions and policies are focused on specific groups of voters and interest groups. The opposite of 'wholesale politics' is 'retail politics': strategies aimed at selling a candidate and policies to a broad, mass audience.

Wilson, Woodrow (1856–1924) Twenty-eighth **President** of the United States, holding office between 1913 and 1921. Born in Virginia, and raised in Georgia and the Carolinas during the **civil war**, Wilson briefly practised law before studying history and political science. His doctoral thesis on Congressional government was highly regarded at the time. Wilson built a successful academic career, becoming President of Princeton University in 1902. Nine years later he successfully ran as the **Democratic Party** candidate for **Governor** of New Jersey, and then became President of the United Sates in 1913.

Wilson's two terms in office are characterised by his progressive domestic reform programme, and the leadership he demonstrated in foreign affairs. At home, Wilson successfully built a Congressional coalition to pass a number of reforms. He reduced tariffs on imported goods, benefiting consumers; he attacked the monopolies of big corporations via the 1914 Anti-Trust Act; he introduced legislation forcing businesses to recognise labour unions and improve conditions for their workers; and he provided lower-interest loans for poorer farmers.

Abroad, President Wilson took a more interventionist line than many of his predecessors. He used military force in Mexico, Haiti and Santa Domingo to protect US interests. His biggest decision in foreign affairs, however, involved US entry to the First World War in 1917. The US expeditionary force under General John J. Pershing broke the stalemate on the western front, bringing the armistice of 1918. It would be Wilson's 'fourteen points' that laid the basis of the Treaty of Versailles that officially ended this war, and he was instrumental in creating the League of Nations. Ironically, the United States did not sign the Versailles Treaty or join the League of Nations. Wilson could not get the consent of the **Republican Party**-controlled **Congress** at home, which took an **isolationist** stance, and failed to ratify these treaties. The United States signed a separate peace treaty with Germany.

writ of certiorari see **certiorari, writ of**

X

X, Malcolm see **Malcolm X**

Y

Yellow Dog Democrat A staunchly loyal supporter of the **Democratic Party**. The phrase originates from the elections of 1928, when an Alabama senator, Tom Heflin, failed to back a fellow Democratic candidate for **President** of the United States. Loyal Democratic Party supporters, who disagreed with Heflin's decision, apparently swore that they would 'even vote for a yellow dog if it ran on a Democratic ticket'.

***Youngstown Sheet and Tube Company* v. *Sawyer*, 1952** A **Supreme Court** decision that confirmed the limits of the US **President**'s power, even in times of national emergency. At the height of the Korean War, steelworkers nationally were about to strike, their employers having rejected calls for increased wages. Fearing that a cut in the supply of steel would hamper the US military effort in Korea, President Harry S. **Truman** intervened. He effectively nationalised many of the nation's steel mills. This would be a temporary measure, the President made it clear, ensuring continued production whilst workers and employers settled their differences. The mill owners abided by Truman's **executive order**, but challenged its validity in the courts. The case of *Youngstown Sheet and Tube Company* v. *Sawyer* was adjudicated by the Supreme Court. The petitioner, Charles Sawyer, was Truman's Secretary of Commerce.

Sawyer argued that Article Two of the US **constitution** gave the President power to make such an intervention during a national emergency. Additionally the administration stated that as **commander in chief**, the President was entitled to take actions that protected US forces in theatres of war. Youngstown Sheet and Tube conversely questioned the President's ability to seize private property, especially without the authority of a prior act of **Congress**.

The Supreme Court's ruling backed the steel-mill owners. The **opinion** stated that the President had no powers to nationalise private property, even in a national emergency. Such intervention, if it were to be constitutional, would first have to be authorised by Congress. The President had no right to make his own law.

Truman immediately returned the steel mills to their owners, and the strike commenced. A settlement was reached after fifty-three days. The President later claimed that the strike had indeed caused some shortages in ammunition available to troops in Korea.

Z

Zipper-gate see **Lewinsky, Monica**

Presidents and Vice Presidents of the United States

Term	President	President's party	Vice President
1789–1793	George Washington	None	John Adams
1793–1797	George Washington	None	John Adams
1797–1801	John Adams	Federalist	Thomas Jefferson
1801–1805	Thomas Jefferson	Dem-Rep	Aaron Burr
1805–1809	Thomas Jefferson	Dem-Rep	George Clinton
1809–1813	James Madison	Dem-Rep	George Clinton (*died in office, 1812*) no VP
1813–1817	James Madison	Dem-Rep	Elbridge Gerry (*died in office, 1814*) no VP
1817–1821	James Monroe	Dem-Rep	Daniel D. Tompkins
1821–1825	James Monroe	Dem-Rep	Daniel D. Tompkins
1825–1829	John Quincy Adams	Dem-Rep	John C. Calhoun
1829–1833	Andrew Jackson	Dem	John C. Calhoun (*resigned, 1832*) no VP
1833–1837	Andrew Jackson	Dem	Martin Van Buren
1837–1841	Martin Van Buren	Dem	Richard M. Johnson
1841–1845	William Henry Harrison (*died in office, 1841*)	Whig	John Tyler (*became President, 1841*)
	John Tyler	Whig	no VP

Term	President	President's party	Vice President
1845–1849	James Knox Polk	Dem	George M. Dallas
1849–1853	Zachary Taylor (*died in office, 1850*)	Whig	Millard Fillmore (*became President, 1850*)
	Millard Fillmore	Whig	no VP
1853–1857	Franklin Pierce	Dem	William R. King (*died in office, 1853*) no VP
1857–1861	James Buchanan	Dem	John C. Breckinridge
1861–1865	Abraham Lincoln	Rep	Hannibal Hamlin
1865–1869	Abraham Lincoln (*assassinated, 1865*)	Rep	Andrew Johnson (*became President, 1865*)
	Andrew Johnson	Dem/Union	no VP
1869–1873	Ulysses S. Grant	Rep	Schuyler Colfax
1873–1877	Ulysses S. Grant	Rep	Henry Wilson (*died in office, 1875*) no VP
1877–1881	Rutherford B. Hayes	Rep	William A. Wheeler
1881–1885	James Abram Garfield (*assassinated, 1881*)	Rep	Chester A. Arthur (*became President, 1881*)
	Chester Alan Arthur	Rep	no VP
1885–1889	Grover Cleveland	Dem	Thomas A. Hendricks (*died in office, 1885*) no VP
1889–1893	Benjamin Harrison	Rep	Levi P. Morton
1893–1897	Grover Cleveland	Dem	Adlai E. Stevenson
1897–1901	William McKinley	Rep	Garret A. Hobart (*died in office, 1899*) no VP
1901–1905	William McKinley (*assassinated, 1901*)	Rep	Theodore Roosevelt (*became President, 1901*)
	Theodore Roosevelt		no VP

Term	President	President's party	Vice President
1905–1909	Theodore Roosevelt	Rep	Charles W. Fairbanks
1909–1913	William Howard Taft	Rep	James S. Sherman (*died in office, 1912*) no VP
1913–1917	Woodrow Wilson	Dem	Thomas R. Marshall
1917–1921	Woodrow Wilson	Dem	Thomas R. Marshall
1921–1925	Warren G. Harding (*died in office, 1923*)	Rep	Calvin Coolidge (*became President, 1923*)
	Calvin Coolidge	Rep	no VP
1925–1929	Calvin Coolidge	Rep	Charles G. Dawes
1929–1933	Herbert Clark Hoover	Rep	Charles Curtis
1933–1937	Franklin D. Roosevelt	Dem	John N. Garner
1937–1941	Franklin D. Roosevelt	Dem	John N. Garner
1941–1945	Franklin D. Roosevelt	Dem	Henry A. Wallace
1945–1949	Franklin D. Roosevelt (*died in office, 1945*)	Dem	Harry S. Truman (*became President, 1945*)
	Harry S. Truman	Dem	no VP
1949–1953	Harry S. Truman	Dem	Alben W. Barkley
1953–1957	Dwight D. Eisenhower	Rep	Richard M. Nixon
1957–1961	Dwight D. Eisenhower	Rep	Richard M. Nixon
1961–1965	John F. Kennedy (*assassinated, 1963*)	Dem	Lyndon B. Johnson (*became President, 1963*)
	Lyndon B. Johnson	Dem	no VP
1965–1969	Lyndon B. Johnson	Dem	Hubert H. Humphrey

Term	President	President's party	Vice President
1969–1973	Richard M. Nixon	Rep	Spiro T. Agnew, 1969–73 (no VP, 10 Oct. 1973 –6 Dec. 1973) Gerald R. Ford, 1973–4
1973–1977	Richard Nixon (*resigned, 1974*)	Rep	Spiro T. Agnew (*resigned from office, 1973*)
	Gerald R. Ford		Gerald R. Ford *became President, 1974*) Nelson A. Rockefeller
1977–1981	Jimmy Carter	Dem	Walter F. Mondale
1981–1985	Ronald Reagan	Rep	George H. W. Bush
1985–1989	Ronald Reagan	Rep	George H. W. Bush
1989–1993	George Bush	Rep	J. Danforth Quayle
1993–1997	Bill Clinton	Dem	Albert A. Gore
1997–2001	Bill Clinton	Dem	Albert A. Gore
2001–2005	George W. Bush	Rep	Richard B. Cheney
2005–	George W. Bush	Rep	Richard B. Cheney

Chief Justices of the United States

John Jay	1789–1795
John Rutledge	1795
Oliver Ellsworth	1796–1800
John Marshall	1801–1835
Roger B. Taney	1836–1864
Salmon P. Chase	1864–1873
Morrison R. Waite	1874–1888
Melville W. Fuller	1888–1910
Edward D. White	1910–1921
William H. Taft	1921–1930
Charles E. Hughes	1930–1941
Harlan F. Stone	1941–1946
Fred M. Vinson	1946–1953
Earl Warren	1953–1969
Warren E. Burger	1969–1986
William H. Rehnquist	1986–2005
John Roberts	2005–

Historic Strength of Political Parties within the US Federal Government

Congress	Period	Majority party in the Senate	Majority party in the House	Party holding the presidency
1st	1789–1791	–	–	–
2nd	1791–1793	F	F	–
3rd	1793–1795	F	DR	F
4th	1795–1797	F	F	F
5th	1797–1799	F	F	F
6th	1799–1801	F	F	F
7th	1801–1803	DR	DR	DR
8th	1803–1805	DR	DR	DR
9th	1805–1807	DR	DR	DR
10th	1807–1809	DR	DR	DR
11th	1809–1811	DR	DR	DR
12th	1811–1813	DR	DR	DR
13th	1813–1815	DR	DR	DR
14th	1815–1817	DR	DR	DR
15th	1817–1819	DR	DR	DR
16th	1819–1821	DR	DR	DR
17th	1821–1823	DR	DR	DR
18th	1823–1825	DR	DR	DR
19th	1825–1827	–	–	C
20th	1827–1829	JD	JD	C
21st	1829–1831	D	D	D
22nd	1831–1833	D	D	D
23rd	1833–1835	D	D	D
24th	1835–1837	D	D	D

Congress	Period	Majority party in the Senate	Majority party in the House	Party holding the presidency
25th	1837–1839	D	D	D
26th	1839–1841	D	D	D
27th	1841–1843	W	W	W
28th	1843–1845	W	D	W
29th	1845–1847	D	D	D
30th	1847–1849	D	W	D
31st	1849–1851	D	D	W
32nd	1851–1853	D	D	W
33rd	1853–1855	D	D	D
34th	1855–1857	D	R	D
35th	1857–1859	D	D	D
36th	1859–1861	D	R	D
37th	1861–1863	R	R	R
38th	1863–1865	R	R	R
39th	1865–1867	U	U	R
40th	1867–1869	R	R	R
41st	1869–1871	R	R	R
42nd	1871–1873	R	R	R
43rd	1873–1875	R	R	R
44th	1875–1877	R	D	R
45th	1877–1879	R	D	R
46th	1879–1881	D	D	R
47th	1881–1883	R	D	R
48th	1883–1885	R	D	R
49th	1885–1887	R	D	D
50th	1887–1889	R	D	D
51st	1889–1891	R	R	R
52nd	1891–1893	R	D	R
53rd	1893–1895	D	D	D
54th	1895–1897	R	R	D
55th	1897–1899	R	R	R
56th	1899–1901	R	R	R
57th	1901–1903	R	R	R
58th	1903–1905	R	R	R
59th	1905–1907	R	R	R
60th	1907–1909	R	R	R

Congress	Period	Majority party in the Senate	Majority party in the House	Party holding the presidency
61st	1909–1911	R	R	R
62nd	1911–1913	R	D	R
63rd	1913–1915	D	D	D
64th	1915–1917	D	D	D
65th	1917–1919	D	D	D
66th	1919–1921	R	R	D
67th	1921–1923	R	R	R
68th	1923–1925	R	R	R
69th	1925–1927	R	R	R
70th	1927–1929	R	R	R
71st	1929–1931	R	R	R
72nd	1931–1933	R	D	R
73rd	1933–1935	D	D	D
74th	1935–1937	D	D	D
75th	1937–1939	D	D	D
76th	1939–1941	D	D	D
77th	1941–1943	D	D	D
78th	1943–1945	D	D	D
79th	1945–1947	D	D	D
80th	1947–1949	R	R	D
81st	1949–1951	D	D	D
82nd	1951–1953	D	D	D
83rd	1953–1955	R	R	R
84th	1955–1957	D	D	R
85th	1957–1959	D	D	R
86th	1959–1961	D	D	R
87th	1961–1963	D	D	D
88th	1963–1965	D	D	D
89th	1965–1967	D	D	D
90th	1967–1969	D	D	D
91st	1969–1971	D	D	R
92nd	1971–1973	D	D	R
93rd	1973–1975	D	D	R
94th	1975–1977	D	D	R
95th	1977–1979	D	D	D
96th	1979–1981	D	D	D

Congress	Period	Majority party in the Senate	Majority party in the House	Party holding the presidency
97th	1981–1983	R	D	R
98th	1983–1985	R	D	R
99th	1985–1987	R	D	R
100th	1987–1989	D	D	R
101st	1989–1991	D	D	R
102nd	1991–1993	D	D	R
103rd	1993–1995	D	D	D
104th	1995–1997	R	R	D
105th	1997–1999	R	R	D
106th	1999–2001	R	R	D
107th	2001–2003	D	R	R
108th	2003–2005	R	R	R
109th	2005–2007	R	R	R

Party abbreviations

- – No distinct party majority
- C coalition
- D Democratic
- DR Democratic-Republican
- F Federalist
- JD Jacksonian Democrat
- R Republican
- U Unionist
- W Whig